Richard Meier

Philip Jodidio

Benedikt Taschen

PAGE 2/SEITE 2:
Richard Meier, 1991
Photo: Luca Vignelli

This book was printed on 100 % chlorine-free bleached paper in accordance with the TCF-standard

© 1995 Richard Meier
Edited by Angelika Muthesius, Cologne
Designed by Mark Thomson, London; Angelika Muthesius, Cologne
Cover design: Massimo Vignelli, New York
German translation: Antje Pehnt, Cologne
French translation: Annie Berthold, Düsseldorf

Printed in Germany
ISBN 3–8228–9256–4

Contents Inhalt Sommaire

"Light is Life" Frank Stella

Douglas House, Harbor Springs, Michigan, 1971–1973

The Atheneum, New Harmony, Indiana, 1975–1979

Recent architecture and art have been marked by frequent stylistic shifts. Indeed, as the century closes, with no dominant aesthetic view, the very idea of style has been called into question. Architecture, once a symbol of permanence has wavered between superficial historical pastiche and a "deconstruction" which tends toward the ephemeral. Few mature creators have passed through this period without being tempted by one or another of the fashions of the times. Fewer still have set and maintained a clear course. In fact, an architect or an artist with a style recognizable over the years is exposed to accusations of immobility or inability to change. Yet many of the most durable works of art were born of rules as strict as the unity of time and place of the classical theater. Few would argue that Shakespeare's adherence to Elizabethan parameters prevented him from encompassing the entire range of human experience in his plays.

Richard Meier, born in Newark, New Jersey in 1934, has been one of the most consistent of contemporary architects, to a point that his stylistic choices, from white enamel panels to nautical railings, are among the most recognizable of his profession. Beneath these surface elements, Meier's plans call on a geometric vocabulary, often based on the circle and the square. Linking the plan to the surface, a rigorous system of grids, even more than the choice of white cladding, constitutes the signature of a Richard Meier building. The rigor of the design is emphasized through meticulous attention to detail, which in turn conveys an impression of quality often lacking in modern construction. Clearly, an approach to architecture that verges on the mathematical could very easily become repetitive, or worse, inhumane. Meier has been accused of just such lack of concern for the inhabitant, yet it seems clear that his precisionist geometric penchant is not so much an expression of formal concerns as it is a means to an end. That end is to create a space where light is

In letzter Zeit haben Architektur und Kunst immer wieder stilistische Umschwünge erlebt. Nun, gegen Ende des Jahrhunderts, hat keine ästhetische Position die Oberhand, und sogar der Begriff des Stils wird in Frage gestellt. Die Architektur, einst ein Symbol des Dauerhaften, schwankt zwischen oberflächlicher historischer Imitation und einer »Dekonstruktion«, die zur Kurzlebigkeit tendiert. Nur wenige selbstbewußte Künstler dieser Zeit widerstanden der Versuchung, dem einen oder anderen modischen Trend zu folgen. Noch wenigere schlugen einen klaren Kurs ein und blieben dabei. Tatsächlich muß sich ein Architekt oder Künstler, dessen Handschrift über Jahre hinweg identifizierbar bleibt, den Vorwurf der Unbeweglichkeit gefallen lassen. Dennoch entstanden viele bleibende Kunstwerke nach Regeln, die so strikt sind wie die Einheit von Zeit und Ort beim klassischen Theater. Kaum einer würde argumentieren, daß das Festhalten an elisabethanischen Traditionen Shakespeare daran hinderte, in seine Stücke die gesamte Skala menschlicher Erfahrungen einzubringen.

Richard Meier, 1934 in Newark, New Jersey, geboren, ist einer der beständigsten Architekten unserer Zeit. Seine stilistischen Merkmale, von den weißen Emailplatten bis zu den Schiffsgeländern, haben in seinem Metier einen überaus hohen Erkennungswert. Abgesehen von diesen äußerlichen Elementen verwendet Meier bei seinen Grundrissen ein geometrisches Vokabular, das häufig auf dem Kreis und dem Quadrat beruht. Die Signatur eines Richard-Meier-Gebäudes besteht weniger in der weißen Verkleidung als in der Verbindung von Grundriß und Fassade durch ein rigoroses Rastersystem. Die Strenge des Entwurfs wird durch eine sorgfältige Behandlung der Details betont, die ihrerseits einen Eindruck von Qualität vermitteln, wie er sich im modernen Bauen selten findet. Natürlich könnte eine Architektur, die ans Mathematische grenzt, leicht repetitiv oder – noch schlimmer – inhuman werden. Tatsächlich ist Meier beschuldigt worden, sich für den Bewohner wenig zu interessieren. Doch sein Hang zur präzisen Geometrie ist offensichtlich weniger ein Ausdruck formaler Vorlieben als Mittel zum Zweck. Der Zweck besteht darin, einen Raum zu schaffen, in dem Licht ein allgegenwärtiges Element ist und seinerseits die Umgebung formt. Architektur soll ein Gefühl des Wohlbefindens bewirken, das im besten Falle eine spirituelle Dimension annehmen kann. Mit den Worten des Künstlers Frank Stella, eines guten Freundes des Architekten: »Licht ist Leben.«

Warum ist Weiß die Farbe Richard Meiers? Seine

L'architecture et l'art ont connu à notre époque de fréquents changements d'orientation stylistiques. Ainsi, en ce siècle finissant marqué par l'absence d'une vision esthétique dominante, c'est l'idée même de style qui a été remise en question. L'architecture, autrefois symbole de permanence, a oscillé entre le pastiche historique superficiel et la «déconstruction» tendant vers l'éphémère. Peu de créateurs en pleine maturité ont traversé cette période sans s'être laissé tenter par l'une ou l'autre des modes de ce temps. Moins encore ont trouvé leur voie et ont réussi à la conserver. En fait, un architecte ou un artiste dont le style n'a pas varié des années durant se verra accusé d'immobilisme ou d'incapacité à évoluer. Pourtant, de nombreuses œuvres d'art parmi les plus durables sont nées de règles strictes comme celle de l'unité de temps et de lieu du théâtre classique. Le fait d'être tenu par les paramètres de l'ère élisabéthaine n'a pas empêché Shakespeare de traiter tout l'éventail des expériences humaines dans ses pièces de théâtre.

Richard Meier, né en 1934 à Newark dans le New Jersey, est l'un des architectes les plus cohérents de notre époque, au point que ses choix stylistiques, des panneaux métalliques en émail blanc aux balustrades façon paquebot, comptent parmi les plus connus de la profession. Sous ces éléments de surface, les plans de Meier font appel à un vocabulaire géométrique basé essentiellement sur le cercle et le carré. Plus encore que le choix typologique du blanc pour les façades, c'est le système rigoureux de grilles, liant le plan à la surface, qui constitue la véritable «signature» d'une construction de Meier. La rigueur du dessin est soulignée par le soin méticuleux accordé au traitement des détails, donnant ainsi une impression de qualité qui fait souvent défaut dans les constructions modernes. Il est certain qu'une approche quasi mathématique de l'architecture pourrait se révéler vite répétitive ou, pire encore, inhumaine. Le principal grief qui a été fait à Meier, c'est justement de ne pas mettre assez de dimension «humaniste» dans son architecture, mais son penchant pour la précision géométrique est moins l'expression de simples préoccupations formelles qu'un moyen d'arriver à une fin. L'objectif de Meier est en effet de créer un espace dans lequel la lumière, élément omniprésent, forme lui-même l'environnement et où l'architecture crée un sentiment de bien-être pouvant atteindre à une dimension spirituelle. «La lumière, c'est la vie», comme l'exprime un ami de l'architecte, le peintre Frank Stella.

Pourquoi le choix de Richard Meier s'est-il porté sur le blanc? C'est lui qui répond le mieux à cette

The Atheneum, New Harmony, Indiana, 1975–1979

an omnipresent element which itself forms the environment, where the architecture creates a feeling of well-being which may, at its best, attain a spiritual dimension. In the words of the architect's good friend, the artist Frank Stella, "Light is life."

Why is white the color of Richard Meier's choice? His own words answer this question best, explain the link between his method and his fundamental concerns, and betray a poetic nature: "White is the ephemeral emblem of perpetual movement. The white is always present but never the same, bright and rolling in the day, silver and effervescent under the full moon of New Year's Eve. Between the sea of consciousness and earth's vast materiality lies this ever-changing line of white. White is the light, the medium of understanding and transformative power."

Early Years

Richard Meier attended Columbia High School in Maplewood, New Jersey, a peaceful suburban town, and went on to Cornell in 1952. Meier has said that "Cornell was very free and open without any dominant influence, and I think that that was the good thing about it. It was left up to the students and what they were interested in, to take advantage of a wide variety of opportunities for learning." A literature course taught by Vladimir Nabokov, and lectures by Alan Solomon, who was later to become the director of the Jewish Museum in New York, on Henri Matisse and Pablo Picasso seem to have particularly marked him. Subsequent to his graduation from Cornell, Meier traveled through Europe, and had occasion to meet Le Corbusier in France. This early admiration for the Swiss-born master would seem to justify the frequent comparisons made between Meier's own work and that of Le Corbusier. As he said himself years later, "I could obviously not create the buildings I do without knowing and loving the work of Corb. Le Corbusier has been a great influence on my mode of creating space."

Before opening his own office in 1963, Richard Meier worked briefly for Davis, Brody & Wisniewski (1959); Skidmore, Owings & Merrill (1960); and Marcel Breuer in New York (1961–1963). Marcel Breuer was one of the great figures of Modernism, or the International Style, as it came to be known after the 1931 exhibition at The Museum of Modern Art, and the book by Henry-Russell Hitchcock and Philip Johnson. Breuer taught with László Moholy-Nagy at the Dessau Bauhaus, and arrived in the United States in the late 1930s like Walter Gropius, Mies van der Rohe and Josef Albers. Their ideas

eigenen Worte beantworten diese Frage am besten, erklären die Verbindung zwischen seiner Methodik und seinen Grundsätzen und verraten eine poetische Natur: »Weiß ist das vergängliche Symbol ständiger Bewegung. Weiß ist immer gegenwärtig, aber nie gleich, hell und unstet am Tage, silbrig und schäumend unter dem Vollmond der Silvester-nacht. Zwischen dem Meer des Bewußtseins und der schweren Stofflichkeit der Erde liegt diese ewig wechselnde Linie des Weiß. Weiß ist das Licht, ein Medium der Verständigung und der Wandlungskraft.«

Frühe Jahre

Richard Meier besuchte die Columbia High School in Maplewood, New Jersey, einer friedlichen Kleinstadt, und ging 1952 zur Cornell University. Er sagte darüber: »Cornell war sehr frei und offen, ohne irgendwelche dominierenden Einflüsse, und ich glaube, das war das Gute daran. Es stand den Studenten je nach ihren Interessen frei, eine große Vielfalt von Möglichkeiten für das Lernen zu nutzen.« Besonders beeindruckten ihn offenbar ein Literaturkurs bei Vladimir Nabokov und Vorlesungen Alan Solomons, dem späteren Direktor des Jewish Museum in New York, über Henri Matisse und Pablo Picasso. Nach seinem Abschluß in Cornell reiste Meier durch Europa und hatte Gelegenheit, Le Corbusier in Frankreich zu begegnen. Diese frühe Bewunderung für den aus der Schweiz stammenden Meister rechtfertigt vielleicht die häufigen Vergleiche zwischen Meiers eigenem Werk und dem Le Corbusiers. Er selbst sagte Jahre später: »Ich könnte meine Bauten zweifellos nicht entwerfen, ohne Corbus Arbeit zu kennen und zu lieben. Le Corbusier hat starken Einfluß auf meine Art, Räume zu bilden, ausgeübt.«

Bevor er 1963 sein eigenes Büro eröffnete, hatte Meier für kurze Zeit bei Davis, Brody & Wisniewski (1959), Skidmore, Owings & Merrill (1960) und Marcel Breuer in New York (1961–1963) gearbeitet. Marcel Breuer war eine der großen Figuren der Moderne oder des Internationalen Stils, wie es nach der Ausstellung im Museum of Modern Art von 1931 und nach dem Buch von Henry-Russell Hitchcock und Philip Johnson hieß. Breuer hatte mit László Moholy-Nagy am Dessauer Bauhaus gelehrt und war wie Walter Gropius, Mies van der Rohe und Josef Albers in den späten dreißiger Jahren nach Amerika gekommen. Ihre Ideen bezogen sich noch auf die sozialen Verhältnisse der Weimarer Republik, und die Pläne des Bauhauses für die Verbesserung der Menschheit durch Architektur und Design waren in den Vereinigten

question, expliquant le lien entre sa méthode et ses préoccupations et révélant ainsi une âme de poète: «Le blanc est l'emblème éphémère du mouvement perpétuel. Le blanc est toujours présent mais n'est jamais le même, brillant et ondoyant dans la clarté du jour, argent et effervescent sous les rayons de la pleine lune au nouvel an. Entre l'océan de la conscience et l'immense matérialité de la terre s'étire la ligne toujours mouvante du blanc. Le blanc, c'est la lumière, le médium de la compréhension et du pouvoir transformateur.»

Les débuts

Après avoir fréquenté la Columbia High School de Maplewood, tranquille commune du New Jersey, Richard Meier entreprend des études à l'université de Cornell en 1952. Selon lui, «Cornell était libéral et ouvert, sans influence dominante, et à mon avis, c'était là son bon côté. Il ne tenait qu'aux étudiants de profiter de la grande variété des cours en fonction de ce qui les intéressait.» Il suit un cours de littérature de Vladimir Nabokov et des conférences sur Henri Matisse et Pablo Picasso données par Alan Solomon, qui deviendra plus tard le directeur du Jewish Museum de New York, et il en sort profondément marqué. Ses études achevées, Meier voyage à travers l'Europe et a l'occasion de rencontrer Le Corbusier en France. L'admiration qu'il voue très tôt au maître suisse semble justifier les comparaisons fréquentes qui ont été faites entre son œuvre et celle de Le Corbusier. Il dira lui-même plus tard: «Je ne pourrais évidemment pas créer mes constructions sans connaître ni aimer le travail de Corbu. Le Corbusier a eu une grande influence sur mon mode de création de l'espace.»
Avant d'ouvrir sa propre agence d'architecture en 1963, Richard Meier exerce quelque temps chez Davis, Brody & Wisniewski (1959), chez Skidmore, Owings & Merrill (1960) et enfin chez Marcel Breuer à New York (1961–1963). Marcel Breuer est l'une des grandes figures du mouvement moderne, ou du Style international, dénommé ainsi après l'exposition de 1931 au Museum of Modern Art de New York et la publication du livre de Henry-Russell Hitchcock et de Philip Johnson. Breuer enseigne d'abord au Bauhaus de Dessau aux côtés de László Moholy-Nagy, puis part pour les Etats-Unis à la fin des années trente, à l'instar de Walter Gropius, Mies van der Rohe et Josef Albers. Leurs idées s'inséraient dans le climat social et idéologique de l'Allemagne de la république de Weimar, mais dans un pays comme les Etats-Unis, le grand dessein du Bauhaus de faire progresser le genre humain par l'architecture et le design perdait inévi-

were related to the social conditions in Weimar Germany, and inevitably Bauhaus schemes for the improvement of mankind through architecture and design seemed less pertinent in the United States. Through their teaching, Gropius at Harvard, Mies at the Illinois Institute of Technology, and through structures such as the Seagram Building (1957) or Breuer's Whitney Museum (1963–1966) they did, however, bring the forms of Modernism to the New World. As Richard Meier has said, "Breuer was not influential although I worked for him for a while," a statement which seems to be borne out by the style of his early work. It does seem clear, however, that Richard Meier and most other American architects of his generation did take as their point of departure the radically simplified designs introduced by the Bauhaus pioneers and other seminal European figures like Le Corbusier.

Art and Architecture

Richard Meier's early and consistent interest in other art forms signals a difference of approach from certain of his colleagues. As early as 1959, he worked in the studio of the painter Frank Stella and participated with the artist in a competition to design a fountain in Philadelphia. Subsequently the two worked on other collaborative projects such as a 1981 exhibition organized by The Architectural League. Stella though, is an artist who always had a pronounced interest in the use of space, from the polygonal canvases he created beginning in 1963, to the sculptural forms of his Indian Bird series in the late 1970s, and finally, in the 1980s, to his interest in creating architecture himself. Space was thus a natural ground of understanding between Richard Meier and Frank Stella. In 1963, Meier was also involved in the design of an exhibition on synagogue architecture at the Jewish Museum in New York, where Alan Solomon introduced him to the painter Barnett Newman. Meier assisted the painter in the preparation of a model of a synagogue he had designed. The architect's interest in art, also manifested by his activity as a painter and a creator of collages, has undoubtedly drawn him more toward the design of museums, and such early projects as his 1967 rehabilitation of the Westbeth Artists' Housing, at the west edge of Greenwich Village in New York. More recently, Richard Meier has clarified his feeling about the difference between the architecture of artists and that of architects; "As an architect you have built in judgments about entry, about accessibility, about movement, about how a structure might be inhabited, rather than being simply concerned about the

Stella Studio and Apartment, New York, 1965

Studio und Appartement Stella, New York, 1965

Studio et appartement de Stella, New York, 1965

Staaten zwangsläufig weitaus weniger relevant. Dennoch führten sie durch ihre Lehrtätigkeit – Gropius in Harvard, Mies am Illinois Institute of Technology – und durch Bauten wie das Seagram Building (1957) oder Breuers Whitney Museum (1963–1966) die Formen der Moderne in die Neue Welt ein. Richard Meier bemerkte: »Breuer hat keinen Einfluß auf mich ausgeübt, obwohl ich eine Zeitlang für ihn gearbeitet habe«, eine Feststellung, die sein Frühwerk zu bestätigen scheint. Andererseits ist offensichtlich, daß Richard Meier und die meisten anderen amerikanischen Architekten seiner Generation jene radikal vereinfachten Entwürfe als Ausgangspunkt nahmen, die auf die Pioniere des Bauhauses und andere wichtige Architekten in Europa wie Le Corbusier zurückgingen.

Kunst und Architektur

Richard Meiers frühes und anhaltendes Interesse an anderen Kunstformen unterscheidet ihn von vielen Kollegen. Schon 1959 arbeitete er im Atelier des Malers Frank Stella und nahm mit dem Künstler an einem Wettbewerb für einen Brunnen in Philadelphia teil. Danach arbeiteten die beiden an weiteren Gemeinschaftsprojekten zusammen, wie an einer Ausstellung von 1981, die von der Architectural League organisiert wurde. Stella ist freilich ein Künstler, der schon immer ein ausgeprägtes Interesse am Räumlichen hatte, von den polygonalen Bildern, die er ab 1963 malte, bis hin zu den skulpturalen Formen seiner Serie »Indian Bird« in den späten siebziger Jahren und schließlich zu seinen eigenen architektonischen Versuchen in den achtziger Jahren. Das Thema des Raums war also für Meier und Stella eine natürliche Basis der Verständigung. 1963 war Meier auch an der Planung einer Ausstellung über Synagogenarchitektur im Jewish Museum in New York beteiligt, wo Alan Solomon ihn mit dem Maler Barnett Newman bekanntmachte. Meier half dem Maler bei der Vorbereitung eines Synagogenmodells, das er entworfen hatte. Seine Liebe zur Kunst, die sich in seinen Aktivitäten als Maler und Collagist äußerte, führte ihn zweifellos auch zum Entwurf von Museen und so frühen Projekten wie der Sanierung von Westbeth Artists' Housing am Westrand von Greenwich Village in New York (1967). Inzwischen hat Meier seine Gefühle über den Unterschied zwischen Architektur von Künstlern und der von Architekten geklärt: »Als Architekt hat man feste Vorstellungen vom Eingang, von der Zugänglichkeit, von der Zirkulation, von der Bewohnbarkeit eines Gebäudes und setzt sich nicht nur einfach mit Form und Beziehung der Konstruktion oder mit konstruktiven

tablement de sa pertinence. Cependant, leur enseignement – Gropius à Harvard, Mies van der Rohe au Illinois Institute of Technology – et des réalisations telles que le Seagram Building (1957) de Mies van der Rohe ou le Whitney Museum de Breuer (1963–1966) permirent d'introduire les formes du modernisme sur le continent américain. Richard Meier déclara un jour: «Breuer n'eut guère d'influence sur moi, bien que j'eusse travaillé pour lui quelque temps», assertion corroborée par le style de ses premières constructions. Nul doute cependant que Richard Meier et d'autres architectes américains de sa génération n'aient pris pour point de départ les dessins radicalement simplifiés des pionniers du Bauhaus et d'autres figures européennes novatrices telles que Le Corbusier.

Art et architecture

Richard Meier manifeste très tôt un intérêt réel pour d'autres formes d'art, ce en quoi sa démarche le distingue déjà de certains de ses collègues. Dès 1959, il travaille dans l'atelier du peintre Frank Stella et participe avec lui à un concours pour l'édification d'une fontaine à Philadelphie. Ils travaillent ensuite ensemble sur d'autres projets tels que l'exposition organisée par la Architectural League en 1981. Stella est un artiste qui a toujours eu un goût prononcé pour l'utilisation de l'espace, comme le prouvent ses toiles polygonales qu'il crée au début de sa carrière en 1963 ou les formes sculpturales de la série «Indian Bird» de la fin des années soixante-dix ou enfin son intérêt très net pour la création architecturale dans les années quatre-vingt. Ainsi l'espace apparaît comme un terrain d'entente naturel entre Richard Meier et Frank Stella. En 1963 également, Meier participe au projet d'une exposition sur l'architecture de synagogues au Jewish Museum de New York, où Alan Solomon le présente au peintre Barnett Newman. Meier aide ce dernier à réaliser la maquette d'une synagogue qu'il a lui-même dessinée. Son intérêt pour l'art, qui se manifeste aussi par la peinture et le collage, l'a certainement plus attiré vers l'architecture muséale et le genre de ses premières réalisations que vers la rénovation du Westbeth Artists' Housing situé dans la partie ouest de Greenwich Village à New York (1967). Plus récemment, Meier a exposé son sentiment sur la différence entre architecture d'artiste et architecture d'architecte: «En tant qu'architecte, vous construisez en jugeant des besoins fonctionnels tels que l'entrée, l'accessibilité, le mouvement, la façon dont la structure peut être habitée plutôt qu'en vous souciant simplement de la forme et du rapport de la

Monumental Fountain, competition entry with Frank Stella, Benjamin Franklin Parkway, Philadelphia, Pennsylvania, 1964

Monumentaler Brunnen, Wettbewerbsbeitrag in Zusammenarbeit mit Frank Stella, Benjamin Franklin Parkway, Philadelphia, Pennsylvania, 1964

Fontaine monumentale, projet de concours réalisé en collaboration avec Frank Stella, Benjamin Franklin Parkway, Philadelphie, Pennsylvanie, 1964

"Recent American Synagogue Architecture," exhibition design and organization, The Jewish Museum, New York, 1963

»Recent American Synagogue Architecture«, Ausstellungsdesign und Organisation, The Jewish Museum, New York, 1963

«Recent American Synagogue Architecture» conception et organisation de l'exposition, The Jewish Museum, New York, 1963

form and relationship of the construction, or constructional elements."

Another example of the influences that have gone into the development of Richard Meier's mature style can be seen in the house he designed for his parents in Essex Fells, New Jersey (1963–1965; ill. p.13). As Joseph Rykwert writes, "That small, single-story building has a deep rectangular roof emulating the reveals of the roof and floors at Wright's Falling Water..." Meier himself has said about Wright's masterpiece that, "It had an electrifying effect on me... what was important to me then was the extension of the interior space into the landscape, I mean the 'visual' extension of Falling Water into its surroundings."

Rykwert relates aspects of another early Meier structure, the *Smith House* (Darien, Connecticut, 1965–1967, ill. pp. 50–53) to Le Corbusier's Villa Stein (Garches, France, 1927–1928), but its play of geometric forms might also bring to mind earlier designs by Theo van Doesburg or Gerrit Rietveld. What is astonishing is the number of characteristics of later Meier buildings which are already apparent in the Smith House. Although the cladding is wood rather than the metal panel which appeared in later buildings, there is a bridge to approach the entrance, a closed facade on the entry side, an open one facing the water, and a high, generously glazed living room. White is already Richard Meier's choice in the mid-1960s as used to emphasize the space and light of the Smith House. That white also brought to mind the Purism of Le Corbusier was certainly not an unintentional coincidence, though some associated Meier's clean geometric vocabulary with the *tabula rasa* of Bauhaus modernism. The very fact that such varied references to earlier architecture are made in the case of Richard Meier seems to prove that from the beginning of his career, he was consciously open to a wide range of influences. In the interview he granted for this book, Meier explains his point of view in the debate about sources, and pleads in favor of an analysis based more on space than on historic references:

"Modernism doesn't have to throw out the baby with the bath-water. I don't think that everything has to be conceived as being new and different just for difference's sake. I believe that architecture is related to the past, that the present is related to the past, and that we learn from the past in order to move into the future. Clearly that doesn't mean that everything that is past has no meaning. I think that there are ways of dealing with space and that

Elementen auseinander.« Ein weiteres Beispiel für die Einflüsse, die zur Entwicklung von Meiers reifem Stil beitrugen, ist das Haus, das er 1963–1965 für seine Eltern in Essex Fells, New Jersey, errichtete (Abb. S. 13). Joseph Rykwert schreibt: »Dieses kleine, eingeschossige Gebäude hat ein weit auskragendes Flachdach, das die Zurschaustellung der Dach- und Stockwerksflächen von Frank Lloyd Wrights Falling Water nachahmt...« Meier selbst sagte über Wrights Meisterwerk: »Auf mich hatte es eine elektrisierende Wirkung... Mir war damals die Ausweitung des Innenraums in die Landschaft wichtig, ich meine, die ›visuelle‹ Ausdehnung von Falling Water in die Umgebung.«

Rykwert bringt Aspekte eines anderen frühen Meier-Baus, des *Hauses Smith* (Darien, Connecticut, 1965–1967; Abb. S. 50–53) mit Le Corbusiers Villa Stein in Garches (1927–1928) in Verbindung. Doch das Spiel der geometrischen Formen erinnert auch an frühere Entwürfe von Theo van Doesburg oder Gerrit Rietveld. Erstaunlich ist, wie viele Merkmale späterer Bauten Meiers bereits bei dem Haus Smith zu erkennen sind. Obwohl die Verkleidung aus Holz besteht und nicht aus Metallplatten wie bei späteren Bauten, gibt es hier eine Brücke, die zum Eingang führt, eine geschlossene Fassade an der Eingangsseite, eine offene zum Wasser hin und einen hohen, großzügig verglasten Wohnraum. Weiß war schon in der Mitte der sechziger Jahre die Farbe, mit der er Räumlichkeit und Licht des Hauses Smith hervorhob. Daß die Farbe Weiß auch an den Purismus Le Corbusiers erinnerte, war sicherlich kein Zufall, obwohl manche Kritiker Meiers klares geometrisches Vokabular mit der *tabula rasa* der Bauhaus-Moderne verglichen. Schon die Tatsache, daß bei Meier so vielfältige Bezüge zur früheren Architektur hergestellt werden, macht deutlich, daß er sich bewußt einer breiten Skala von Einflüssen öffnete. In dem Interview, das er für dieses Buch gewährte, erläutert er seinen Standpunkt in der Diskussion über künstlerische Quellen und plädiert für eine Analyse, die eher auf Räumlichkeit als auf historischen Referenzen beruht:

»Der Modernismus muß das Kind nicht mit dem Bad ausschütten. Ich glaube nicht, daß alles neu und anders konzipiert werden sollte, nur, damit es anders ist. Ich denke, die Architektur ist mit der Vergangenheit verbunden, die Gegenwart ist mit der Vergangenheit verbunden, und wir lernen von der Vergangenheit, um uns in die Zukunft zu bewegen. Das heißt natürlich nicht, daß alles, was vergangen ist, keine Bedeutung hat. Ich glaube, es gibt Möglichkeiten, mit dem Raum umzugehen,

construction ou des éléments de construction». Parmi les diverses influences qui ont aidé à l'évolution stylistique de Richard Meier, on en décèle une particulière dans la maison qu'il construisit pour ses parents à Essex Fells, New Jersey (1963–1965; ill. p. 13). Joseph Rykwert écrit: «Cette maison de plain-pied a un toit rectangulaire et profond empruntant beaucoup à la conception inédite du toit et des étages de Falling Water de Wright ...» Richard Meier a avoué lui-même au sujet du chef d'œuvre de Wright: «Il eut un effet électrisant sur moi ... ce qui était alors important pour moi, c'était le prolongement de l'espace intérieur dans le paysage, je veux dire le prolongement «visuel» de Falling Water dans son environnement.»

Rykwert compare aussi certains aspects d'une autre construction de Meier, la *maison Smith* (Darien, Connecticut, 1965–1967; ill. p. 50–53), avec la villa Stein (Garches, France, 1927–1928) de Le Corbusier, mais son jeu de formes géométriques évoque tout aussi bien les dessins de Theo van Doesburg ou de Gerrit Rietveld. Ce qui ne laisse pas de surprendre dans la maison Smith, c'est la présence d'un bon nombre des thèmes récurrents des futures constructions de Meier. Bien que le revêtement soit en bois et pas encore en panneaux de métal, comme c'est le cas dans les réalisations ultérieures, on y trouve déjà le pont menant à l'entrée, la façade fermée du côté de l'entrée, la façade ouverte sur la mer et le salon vitré à double hauteur. Dès le milieu des années soixante, le blanc est un des choix typologiques de Meier pour mettre en valeur l'espace et la lumière. Que le blanc évoque aussi le Purisme de Le Corbusier n'est certainement pas le fruit du hasard même si certains ont vu dans le vocabulaire géométrique pur de Meier un lien avec le langage révolutionnaire du Bauhaus. Le simple fait de se référer à diverses tendances de l'architecture passée pour définir celle de Meier tend à prouver que, dès le début de sa carrière, l'architecte s'est sciemment ouvert à une pluralité d'influences. Meier explique son point de vue personnel dans la discussion sur les sources artistiques, plaidant en faveur d'une analyse fondée plutôt sur l'espace que sur les références historiques:
«Le modernisne ne doit pas pécher par excès de zèle. Je ne crois pas qu'il faille concevoir à tout prix du nouveau et du différent simplement pour rechercher de la différence. Je pense que l'architecture est liée au passé, que le présent est relié au passé et que l'enseignement de ce passé nous permet d'aller vers l'avenir. Cela ne signifie pas

Frank Lloyd Wright: Falling Water, House for Edgar J. Kaufmann, Bear Run, Pennsylvania, 1935–1939

Frank Lloyd Wright: Falling Water, Haus für Edgar J. Kaufmann, Bear Run, Pennsylvania, 1935–1939

Frank Lloyd Wright: Falling Water, maison construite pour Edgar J. Kaufmann, Bear Run, Pennsylvanie, 1935–1939

House for Mr. and Mrs. Jerome Meier, Essex Fells, New Jersey, 1963–1965

Haus für Mr. und Mrs. Jerome Meier, Essex Fells, New Jersey, 1963–1965

Maison construite pour M. et Mme Jerome Meier, Essex Fells, New Jersey, 1963–1965

we can learn from life, I would like to think that I can learn from Bernini and Borromini and Bramante, as well as I can from Le Corbusier, Frank Lloyd Wright and Alvar Aalto. This is what's different about modern architecture today and modern architecture as it grew up in the thirties and forties. What we do is related to the history of architecture. What we do is also unfortunately related to many pragmatic concerns, which don't change overnight, either, and ultimately it's a way in which we make space and deal with the making of space. That's what is important in architecture, not so much the references that might occur."[1]

Fame and the New York Five

Among the early public projects of Richard Meier, the *Bronx Developmental Center* (1970–1977; ill. pp. 54–55), stands out because it represents one of his first large-scale uses of aluminum panels. Intended for physically disabled and mentally retarded children, the Center is located in an industrial area between the Hutchinson River Parkway and railroad tracks. As such, it was difficult to imagine a building that opened out into the environment. Rather, Meier has chosen to close the outside facades in favor of internal courtyards. The reflective aluminum finish of the wall surfaces indeed seems to contribute to the closed appearance of the building. Rather than the rigorous grid patterns toward which he evolved in later projects, the panels here adopt several different formats according to the circumstances, with a full unit measuring 365 x 333 cm. Although sizable, housing 380 together with outpatient facilities, the Bronx Developmental Center brought Richard Meier less notoriety than much smaller individual houses such as the one he built in Harbor Springs, Michigan between 1971 and 1973.

The *Douglas House* (ill. pp. 56–59) owes at least part of its celebrity to its dramatic setting on a steep, wooded site on the shores of Lake Michigan. Related in its design to the Smith House, this home is entered through a bridge at roof level, and in many ways recalls nautical metaphors. It is, in any case, a strikingly incongruous object in this natural setting, a gleaming white jewel shining in the forest. A decade later, the author Tom Wolfe observed the popularity of buildings like this one and wrote:

"Every new $900,000 summer house in the north woods of Michigan or on the shore of Long Island has so many pipe railings, ramps, hob-tread metal spiral stairways, sheets of industrial plate glass, banks of tungsten-halogen lamps and white

View of the southeast facade of the Smith House, Darien, Connecticut, 1965–1967

Ansicht der Südostfassade des Hauses Smith, Darien, Connecticut, 1965–1967

Vue de la façade sud-ouest de la maison Smith, Darien, Connecticut, 1965–1967

und wir können vom Leben lernen. Ich denke, ich kann von Bernini und Borromini und Bramante ebenso lernen, wie ich von Le Corbusier, Frank Lloyd Wright und Alvar Aalto lernen kann. Das ist der Unterschied zwischen der modernen Architektur von heute und der modernen Architektur, wie sie in den dreißiger und vierziger Jahren entstand. Was wir machen, hat mit der Geschichte der Architektur zu tun. Was wir machen, hat leider auch mit vielen pragmatischen Interessen zu tun, die sich leider auch nicht über Nacht ändern, und letztlich geht es darum, wie wir Raum schaffen und mit der Entstehung von Raum umgehen. Das ist das Wichtige in der Architektur, und nicht so sehr die Bezüge, die sich vielleicht ergeben.«[1]

Ruhm und die New York Five

Unter den frühen öffentlichen Projekten Richard Meiers spielt das *Bronx Developmental Center* (1970–1977; Abb. S. 54–55) eine besondere Rolle, weil er hier zum erstenmal Aluminiumplatten in größerem Maßstab verwendete. Das Zentrum ist für körperlich und geistig behinderte Kinder bestimmt und liegt in einem Industriebezirk zwischen dem Hutchinson River Parkway und einem Eisenbahngelände. Insofern war es schwierig, sich ein Gebäude vorzustellen, das sich zur Umgebung öffnete. Stattdessen entschloß sich Meier, die Außenfassaden zugunsten von Innenhöfen zu schließen. Die reflektierende Aluminiumverkleidung der Wandplatten trägt zur umschlossenen Erscheinung des Gebäudes bei. Anstelle der rigorosen Rastermuster, die er bei späteren Projekten entwickelte, haben die Platten hier unterschiedliche Formate, wobei eine volle Einheit 365 x 333 cm mißt. Trotz seiner Größe – 380 Bewohner und zusätzliche ambulante Einrichtungen – hat das Bronx Developmental Center Richard Meier weniger Anerkennung eingebracht als sehr viel kleinere Häuser wie das in Harbor Springs, Michigan.

Das *Haus Douglas* (1971–1973; Abb. S. 56–59) verdankt zumindest einen Teil seiner Berühmtheit seiner dramatischen Lage in einem steilen, bewaldeten Gebiet am Ufer des Michigansees. Ähnlich wie beim Haus Smith sind zahlreiche maritime Metaphern verwendet, und der Zugang führt über eine Brücke auf Dachniveau. Das Haus wirkt in dieser natürlichen Umgebung wie ein überraschender Fremdkörper, ein strahlendes weißes Juwel mitten im Wald. Ein Jahrzehnt später stellte der Autor Tom Wolfe eine Betrachtung über die Popularität von Bauten wie diesem an. Er schrieb:

»Jede Datscha zu $ 900000,– pro Stück in den

évidemment que tout ce qui est passé n'ait aucun sens. Je pense qu'il existe des manières de traiter l'espace et la vie qui peuvent être riches d'enseignement, je crois que je peux en apprendre autant du Bernin, de Borromini ou de Bramante que de Le Corbusier, Frank Lloyd Wright et Alvar Aalto. C'est ce qui différencie l'architecture actuelle de l'architecture issue des années trente et quarante. Ce que nous faisons est étroitement lié à l'histoire de l'architecture. Ce que nous faisons dépend malheureusement aussi de nombreuses préoccupations pragmatiques qui ne changent pas en un jour, et pour moi finalement, c'est une manière de créer de l'espace et d'en mener à bien la réalisation. Voilà ce qui importe vraiment dans l'architecture, pas tellement les références qui pourraient se présenter.»[1]

La renommée et le «New York Five»

Parmi les premiers projets publics réalisés par Richard Meier, le *Bronx Developmental Center* (1970–1977; ill. p. 54–55) occupe une place particulière parce qu'il représente sa première tentative d'utiliser à grande échelle les panneaux d'aluminium. Le centre, où sont placés des enfants handicapés physiques et mentaux, se situe dans une zone industrielle coincée entre le Hutchinson River Parkway et la voie ferrée. Difficile dans ces conditions d'imaginer une construction ouverte sur son environnement. Meier a donc choisi de fermer les façades extérieures et d'ouvrir des cours intérieures. La finition des surfaces murales en aluminium réfléchissant confirme l'impression de clôture extérieure de l'édifice. Au lieu du réseau modulaire rigoureux vers lequel l'architecte évoluera plus tard, les panneaux de cette construction adoptent plusieurs formats correspondant aux divers arrangements de la structure mais avec une unité de base de 365 cm x 333 cm. Bien que de taille respectable et accueillant 380 personnes – patients en consultation externe compris – le Bronx Developmental Center n'a pas donné à Richard Meier la notoriété que certaines de ses réalisations plus petites, comme la belle résidence de Harbor Springs, Michigan, lui valurent.

La *maison Douglas* (1971–1973; ill. p. 56–59) doit sa célébrité, au moins en partie, au site sauvage et insolite sur lequel elle a été édifíée: les rives escarpées et boisées du lac Michigan. Apparentée par son plan à la maison Smith, cette maison dans laquelle on pénètre par une passerelle au niveau du toit évoque à maints égards des images du monde naval. En tout cas, cette construction est

Above and below: detail view of the Bronx Developmental Center, Bronx, New York, 1970–1977

Oben und unten: Detail des Bronx Developmental Center, Bronx, New York, 1970–1977

Ci-dessus et ci-dessous: détail du Bronx Developmental Center, Bronx, New York, 1970–1977

cylindrical shapes, it looks like an insecticide refinery. I once saw the owners of such a place driven to the edge of sensory deprivation by the whiteness & lightness & leanness and cleanness & bareness & spareness of it all. They became desperate for an antidote, such as coziness and color."[2]

While the Douglas House was under construction, in 1972, Meier participated in a book entitled "Five Architects", together with Peter Eisenman, Michael Graves, John Hejduk, and Charles Gwathmey. As Wolfe says facetiously, "Their idea was to return to the purest of all the purists, Dr. Purism himself, Le Corbusier, and explore the paths he had indicated. Their Apollinaire was Colin Rowe, a professor of architecture at Cornell who had written an influential exegesis of Le Corbusier's work." Formalist in its ideas, often compared to the Minimalist artists of the period, this group was quickly attacked by such architects as Robert A.M. Stern, who excoriated Colin Rowe for being "stuck in the hothouse aesthetics of the 1920's." The group's rallying call of the time was, "You don't learn about architecture from Las Vegas," a specific reference to Robert Venturi's influential 1972 book "Learning from Las Vegas", sequel to the 1966 manifesto "Complexity and Contradiction in Architecture", which championed "inclusion" and such diverse influences as highway signs and Tom Wolfe's own "Kandy-Colored Tangerine-Flake Streamline Baby", as opposed to the spare whiteness of the newly baptized "New York Five." Indeed much of the debate at this time was led by theoreticians such as Robert Venturi or Peter Eisenman who had very few if any built works to their credit. Graves and Hejduk did more drawing than building, which seemed to confer all the more prestige on them, as opposed to the architects who actually "got their hands dirty." On both sides of this theoretical argument, which opposed a certain type of Modernism to the forerunners of Post-Modernism, there seems to have been much more concern about visual or formal values than a real analysis of the role of architecture in society. The sociological foundations of the modern movement were in any case set aside in favor of matters of aesthetics.

Richard Meier did continue to build. In many ways he remained the most consistent of the New York Five, true to the forms he began to perfect in the 1970s, aware that within a restrained formal vocabulary, a great deal of variety could be found. He seems also to have become increasingly aware of the transfigurative power of architectural space. It is certainly noteworthy that as Resident Architect

nördlichen Wäldern von Michigan oder an der Küste von Long Island hat so viele Stahlrohr-Geländer, Rampen, metallene Wendeltreppen mit genieteten Stufen, verspiegelte Glasflächen, ganze Böschungen aus Wolfram-Halogen-Lampen und weiße zylindrische Formen, daß sie aussieht wie eine Insektizid-Siederei. Ich habe erlebt, wie die Besitzer eines solchen Orts durch dessen Helles & Grelles & Reines & Feines & Leeres & Hehres an den Rand des sinnlichen Entzugskomas getrieben wurden. Verzweifelt suchten sie nach einem Gegengift wie Gemütlichkeit und Farbe.«[2]

1972, als das Haus Douglas noch im Bau war, beteiligte sich Meier an einem Buch mit dem Titel »Five Architects«, zusammen mit Peter Eisenman, Michael Graves, John Hejduk und Charles Gwathmey. Tom Wolfe scherzte: »Sie fanden, man müsse zum pursten aller Puristen zurückkehren, zu Dr. Purismus persönlich, zu Le Corbusier, und die Pfade erkunden, die er bezeichnet hatte. Ihr Apollinaire war Colin Rowe, ein Architekturprofessor in Cornell, der eine einflußreiche Exegese der Werke Le Corbusiers geschrieben hatte.« Wegen ihres Formalismus, der häufig mit dem Minimalismus der Künstler aus der gleichen Zeit verglichen wurde, sah sich die Gruppe schnell den Angriffen von Architekten wie Robert A.M. Stern ausgesetzt. Er warf Colin Rowe vor, er sei »in der Treibhaus-Ästhetik der zwanziger Jahre steckengeblieben«. Meiers Parole war damals: »Von Las Vegas kann man nichts über Architektur lernen« – eine Anspielung, die sich auf Robert Venturis einflußreiches Buch »Learning from Las Vegas« von 1972 (Lernen von Las Vegas) bezog, den Folgeband von »Complexity and Contradiction in Architecture« (Komplexität und Widerspruch in der Architektur) aus dem Jahr 1966. Venturi setzte sich für eine »Einbeziehung« und auch für so unterschiedliche Einflüsse wie Reklameschilder am Highway oder Tom Wolfes »Kandy-Colored Tangerine-Flake Streamline Baby« ein – im Gegensatz zum kargen Weiß der neu gegründeten »New York Five«. Tatsächlich wurde die Diskussion in dieser Zeit überwiegend von Theoretikern wie Venturi oder Peter Eisenman geführt, die sehr wenige oder gar keine eigenen Bauten vorzuweisen hatten. Graves und Hejduk zeichneten mehr, als sie bauten, was ihnen aber offenbar umso mehr Prestige eintrug, weil sie sich nicht wie andere Architekten »die Hände schmutzig machten«. Auf beiden Seiten dieser theoretischen Debatte, die einen gewissen Typus der Moderne den Vorläufern der Postmoderne gegenüberstellte, schien ein sehr viel größeres Interesse an visuellen oder formalen Werten zu herrschen als

un objet d'une incongruité saisissante dans ce cadre naturel, joyau brillant d'une blancheur immaculée dans son écrin forestier. Dix ans plus tard, l'auteur Tom Wolfe, évoquant ce type de maisons, écrira: «Toute nouvelle résidence secondaire à neuf cent mille dollars construite dans une forêt du nord du Michigan ou sur les rives de Long Island a tant de balustrades façon paquebot, de rampes, d'escaliers métalliques en spirale et à marches gironnées, tant de vitrages en verre épais, de rails de lampes halogènes et tungstènes et, enfin, de formes cylindriques blanches qu'elle finit par ressembler à une usine d'insecticides. J'ai connu autrefois les propriétaires d'une de ces maisons; sa blancheur, sa clarté, sa maigreur, sa propreté, sa nudité et son économie les avaient menés au bord du dysfonctionnement sensoriel. Ils souhaitaient désespérément un antidote, quelque chose comme une atmosphère douillette et de la couleur.»[2]

Pendant la construction de la maison Douglas en 1972, Meier écrit un livre intitulé «Five Architects» (Cinq Architectes) en collaboration avec Peter Eisenman, Michael Graves, John Hejduk et Charles Gwathmey. Non sans facétie, voici ce qu'écrit Wolfe sur ce collectif: «Leur idée était de revenir au pur d'entre les purs, Monsieur Purisme en personne, Le Corbusier, et d'explorer les voies qu'il avait tracées. Leur Apollinaire était Colin Rowe, un professeur d'architecture de Cornell, qui avait commis une exégèse remarquée de l'œuvre de Le Corbusier.» En raison de son formalisme, souvent comparé au minimalisme des artistes de cette période, le groupe va bientôt être la cible de certains architectes comme Robert A.M. Stern, qui fustige Colin Rowe pour s'être «enferré dans l'esthétique de serre des années vingt». Le cri de ralliement de Meier à l'époque était: «On ne peut rien apprendre de l'architecture avec Las Vegas», allusion directe au livre phare de Robert Venturi «Learning from Las Vegas» (Apprendre de Las Vegas) publié en 1972. Dans ce livre, une suite au manifeste de 1966 «Complexity and Contradiction in Architecture» (Complexité et contradiction dans l'architecture), Venturi s'était fait le champion de «l'inclusion», d'objets-références tels que les enseignes de la route, et de l'essai de Tom Wolfe «The Kandy-Colored Tangerine-Flake Streamline Baby», par opposition à la blancheur aride prônée par le nouveau groupe des «New York Five». Il est à noter que la discussion était dirigée en partie par des théoriciens tels que Robert Venturi et Peter Eisenman qui n'avaient à leur actif que peu, pour ne pas dire aucune, réalisation architecturale. Graves et Hejduk dessinaient plus qu'ils ne

EISENMAN GRAVES GWATHMEY HEJDUK MEIER

Cover of "Five Architects". Meier participated in this book together with Peter Eisenman, Michael Graves, John Hejduk, and Charles Gwathmey, 1972

Umschlag zu »Five Architects«. Meier beteiligte sich an diesem Buch zusammen mit Peter Eisenman, Michael Graves, John Hejduk und Charles Gwathmey, 1972

Couverture du «Five Architects». Meier a écrit ce livre en collaboration avec Peter Eisenman, Michael Graves, John Hejduk et Charles Gwathmey, 1972

Above and below: two views of The Atheneum, New Harmony, Indiana, 1975–1979

Oben und unten: zwei Ansichten des Atheneum, New Harmony, Indiana, 1975–1979

Ci-dessus et ci-dessous: deux vues de l'Atheneum, New Harmony, Indiana, 1975–1979

at the American Academy in Rome in 1973, he chose to take students to visit the Baroque churches of southern Germany. As Richard Meier has said more recently, regarding the permanence of architecture, "I think that there are ephemeral buildings, certainly World's Fair buildings are for the most part of that type. Certain fast food restaurants on longer highways could be ephemeral. You could get rid of them after a while. I think for the most part architecture is not ephemeral. I think it's much too serious, much too costly, takes much too long, and involves many too many people, to be a throw away."[3] This remark provides a clear indication of just why Meier feels that Las Vegas is not a valid starting point for architectural inspiration.

Utopian Schemes

Richard Meier's architecture certainly took a step forward with his design of *The Atheneum* in New Harmony, Indiana (1975–1979; ill. pp. 60–63). It is here, at the entrance to the best known utopian community in America that his vocabulary and style began to be defined in terms of public architecture. Splendidly isolated and elevated because of the danger of flooding along the Wabash River, this is again a ship, with its prominent nautical railings and its elegant gangplank of an entrance ramp. It is an ark of culture and precision in a largely natural environment, but within there are constant opportunities to see, and admire the exterior. When asked if his architecture could be thought of as a kind of victory over nature, Meier responds:

"No, I think that it's really a statement of what we do as architects, what we make is not natural. I think that the fallacy that Frank Lloyd Wright perpetrated for many years had to do with the nature of materials. He claimed to use what are called natural materials, but the minute you cut down that tree and you use it in construction, it is no longer alive, it is no longer growing, it is inert. The materials we're using in construction are not natural, they are not changing with the seasons, or with the time of day. What we make is static in its material quality. Therefore, it's a counterpoint to nature. Nature is changing all around us, and the architecture should help reflect those changes. I think it should help intensify one's perception of the changing colors of nature, changing colors of the day, rather than attempt to have the architecture change. I've defined a vocabulary of forms which I think are not forms one would find in nature. I think that it's very difficult, if not impossible to make as beautiful forms as those

an einer wirklichen Analyse der Rolle der Architektur in der Gesellschaft.

Richard Meier fuhr fort zu bauen. In mancher Hinsicht war er der beständigste der New York Five. Er blieb den Formen treu, die er seit den siebziger Jahren perfektioniert hatte, denn er war sich darüber im klaren, daß sich auch aus einem beschränkten Formenvokabular eine große Vielfalt entwickeln läßt. Offenbar wurde ihm auch die transformatorische Kraft des architektonischen Raums immer deutlicher bewußt. Typisch für ihn ist sicherlich, daß er 1973 als Gastarchitekt an der American Academy in Rom mit Studenten die Barockkirchen in Süddeutschland besuchte. In jüngerer Zeit sagte Richard Meier über die Permanenz der Architektur: »Ich glaube, es gibt vergängliche Bauten, gewiß gehören die Bauten für Weltausstellungen meist diesem Typus an. Bestimmte Fast-Food-Restaurants an längeren Autobahnen könnten vergänglich sein. Man könnte sie nach einer Weile loswerden. Ich glaube, meist ist Architektur nicht vergänglich. Ich glaube, sie ist viel zu ernsthaft, viel zu kostspielig, braucht zu viel Zeit und schließt zu viele Menschen ein, um ein Wegwerfprodukt zu sein.«[3]

Utopische Projekte

Mit seinem *Atheneum* in New Harmony, Indiana (1975–1979; Abb. S. 60–63), gelang Meier zweifellos ein Schritt vorwärts. Hier, bei der bekanntesten utopischen Gemeinschaft Amerikas, begann er, seine Formensprache zum öffentlichen Bauen hin zu orientieren. Das Gebäude liegt isoliert und wegen der Überschwemmungsgefahr des Wabash River erhöht und ist wiederum ein »Schiff«, mit markanten Schiffsrelings und einer eleganten Gangway als Eingangsrampe. Es ist eine Arche der Kultur und Präzision inmitten einer weitgehend natürlichen Umgebung, doch im Inneren gibt es immer wieder Möglichkeiten, die Landschaft zu bewundern. Auf die Frage, ob sich seine Architektur als eine Art Sieg über die Natur betrachten ließe, antwortete Meier:

»Nein, ich glaube, es ist wirklich ein Statement dessen, was wir als Architekten tun, denn was wir machen, ist nicht natürlich. Ich glaube, der Irrtum, dem Frank Lloyd Wright jahrelang verfallen war, hatte mit der Natur der Materialien zu tun. Er behauptete, er benutze sogenannte natürliche Materialien, aber in der Minute, in der man diesen Baum fällt und beim Bau verwendet, lebt er nicht mehr, wächst nicht mehr, ist er tot. Die Materialien, die wir beim Bauen verwenden, sind nicht natürlich, sie wechseln nicht mit den Jahres- oder

construisaient, ce qui leur conférait un prestige accru par rapport aux architectes qui, eux, «se salissaient les mains». Dans les deux camps de cette joute théorique opposant des tenants du modernisme à des précurseurs du postmodernisme, on paraissait plus se préoccuper de questions visuelles ou formelles que de faire une analyse réelle et profonde du rôle de l'architecture dans la société.

Richard Meier continuait à construire. A maints égards, il restait le plus cohérent des «New York Five», fidèle aux formes qu'il avait perfectionnées dans les années soixante-dix, conscient qu'à l'intérieur même d'un idiome formel restreint on pouvait puiser toute la diversité nécessaire. A cette époque aussi, il semble avoir pris la mesure du pouvoir transfiguratif de l'espace architectural. Il n'est pas inutile de noter que lors de son séjour à Rome comme architecte résident de l'Académie américaine, il emmena des étudiants visiter les églises baroques du sud de l'Allemagne. Il y a peu de temps encore, Richard Meier déclarait au sujet de la permanence de l'architecture: «Je pense qu'il peut y avoir des constructions éphémères, les pavillons de l'Exposition universelle en sont pour la plupart. Certains restaurants fast-food des autoroutes entrent aussi dans cette catégorie. On pourrait s'en débarrasser au bout de quelque temps. Mais, à mon avis, la majeure partie de l'architecture n'a rien d'éphémère. C'est une chose beaucoup trop sérieuse, beaucoup trop coûteuse, qui prend beaucoup trop de temps et qui implique beaucoup de trop de gens pour être un simple produit à jeter.»[3]

Projets utopiques

L'art de Meier connut un tournant décisif avec la réalisation de l'*Atheneum* de New Harmony, Indiana (1975–1979; ill. p. 60–63). C'est là, au seuil d'une des communautés utopiques les plus célèbres des Etats-Unis, que son langage et son style commencent à se définir en termes d'architecture publique. Merveilleusement isolé et posé sur une butte en raison des crues de la rivière Wabash, cet objet architectural ressemble lui aussi à un navire avec ses balustrades façon paquebot et l'élégante passerelle de la rampe d'accès. C'est une arche de culture, un monument de précision dans un environnement en grande partie naturel, mais, de l'intérieur, de constantes échappées visuelles permettent de voir et d'admirer l'extérieur. Quand on lui demande si son architecture peut être considérée comme une victoire sur la nature, Meier répond:

«Non, je pense que c'est réellement l'exposé de

Frank Lloyd Wright:
Atrium of the Solomon R. Guggenheim Museum, New York,
1943–1959

Frank Lloyd Wright:
Atrium des Solomon R. Guggenheim Museum, New York,
1943–1959

Frank Lloyd Wright:
Atrium du Solomon R. Guggenheim Museum, New York,
1943–1959

Atrium of the High Museum of
Art, Atlanta, Georgia, 1980–1983

Atrium des High Museum of Art,
Atlanta, Georgia, 1980–1983

Atrium du High Museum of Art,
Atlanta, Géorgie, 1980–1983

which occur in nature. Nature does it better, but what we can do is conceive forms which are inter-related in a way, and which may not be inter-related in nature. I think that is really what I am trying to do. I am trying to find a form of construction, which has some meaning in human terms, and relates to idea of the place."[4]

A complex repertory of the influences which have played on Meier together with his own areas of predilection are united in the *High Museum of Art* in Atlanta, Georgia (1980–1983; ill. pp. 80–83). Like the Atheneum, it has a long entry ramp, but here the defining volume is undoubtedly the monumental atrium. Having worked on the small Aye Simon Reading Room (1977–1978) at the Guggenheim, Meier had undoubtedly had time to reflect on the strengths and weaknesses of Wright's defining architectural statement. "I learned from the Guggenheim Museum," says the architect, "where you see a work, and then you go around to the other side of the ramp, and when you look across you see it differently." Although the High Museum does indeed offer multiple points of view on the works of art exhibited, it avoids the problems created by Wright's spiral gallery by separating ramps from galleries. "To some extent the light-filled atrium space is inspired by, and a commentary on, the central space of the Guggenheim Museum," concludes Meier.

Expanding on the repertory of curved and rectilinear volumes he had already employed in other projects, Meier defined the atrium of the High Museum as a social gathering place, or cultural center for the southern city. And yet this definition of gathering implies a building which is turned in on itself. The ramp is an invitation extended to passersby, but any gathering must take place in the building's center. Here, as in other instances, Richard Meier buildings have often taken on the appearance of inviolable bastions of perfection, far removed from their surroundings. Although it would be difficult to suggest that his light-flooded volumes project an image of sterility, their perfection, indeed their very whiteness seem to set them apart from the disorder of existence. "I think that the responsibility of an architect," says Richard Meier, "is really to create a sense of order, a sense of place, a sense of relationships. These ideas are inherent in the architecture, and therefore the precision, or the relationships, are very import-ant to me, in making the ideas and the relation-ships as clear as possible, and in creating a sense of order. I'm not interested in creating chaos, others can do that."

Tageszeiten. Was wir machen, ist in seiner mate-riellen Qualität statisch. Deshalb ist es ein Kontra-punkt zur Natur. Um uns herum wandelt sich die Natur, und die Architektur sollte helfen, diese Wandlungen zu reflektieren. Ich glaube, sie sollte helfen, die Wahrnehmung der wechselnden Farben der Natur, der wechselnden Farben des Tages zu schärfen und nicht versuchen, sich selbst zu ver-ändern. Ich habe ein Vokabular entwickelt, dessen Formen, glaube ich, nicht in der Natur vorkom-men. Ich glaube, es ist sehr schwierig, wenn nicht unmöglich, so schöne Formen zu entwickeln wie die, die man in der Natur findet. Die Natur macht es besser, aber das, was wir tun können ist, For-men zu entwerfen, die irgendwie miteinander ver-bunden sind und die in der Natur vielleicht nicht miteinander verbunden sind. Ich glaube, das ist wirklich das, was ich zu tun versuche. Ich versuche, eine neue Form des Bauens zu finden, die irgend-eine menschliche Bedeutung hat und sich auf die Idee des Ortes bezieht.«[4]

Das komplexe Repertoire der Einflüsse, die auf Meier einwirkten, wird ebenso wie seine eigenen Vorlieben im *High Museum of Art* in Atlanta, Georgia (1980–1983; Abb. S. 80–83), sichtbar. Wie das Atheneum hat es eine lange Eingangsrampe, doch das beherrschende Volumen ist hier zweifellos das monumentale Atrium. Nachdem Meier an dem kleinen Aye-Simon-Lesesaal im Guggenheim Museum (1977–1978) gearbeitet hatte, war er sich offenbar über die Stärken und Schwächen von Wrights markantem Gebäude klargeworden. »Ich lernte vom Guggenheim Museum«, sagt der Architekt, »wo man ein Kunstwerk sieht und dann auf die andere Seite der Rampe geht, und wenn man hinüberblickt, sieht man es anders.« Obwohl das High Museum of Art ebenfalls vielfältige Perspektiven der ausgestellten Kunstwerke bietet, vermeidet es die Probleme von Wrights Spiralform, indem es die Rampen von den Ausstellungsräumen trennt.
»Bis zu einem gewissen Grade ist der lichterfüllte Atriumbereich vom Zentralraum des Guggenheim Museum inspiriert und ein Kommentar dazu«, bemerkt Meier.

Von den gekurvten und rechtwinkligen Volumen ausgehend, die er bereits bei anderen Projekten angewandt hatte, definierte Meier das Atrium des High Museum als Versammlungsort oder Kultur-zentrum des südlichen Stadtteils. Seine Auffas-sung von einem Versammlungsort setzt freilich ein Gebäude voraus, das nach innen orientiert ist. Die Rampe ist eine Einladung an die Passanten, doch jede Veranstaltung muß im Inneren stattfinden.

ce que nous faisons en tant qu'architectes, ce que nous construisons n'est pas naturel. L'erreur commise par Wright, il y a déjà longtemps, portait sur la nature des matériaux. Il prétendait utiliser des matériaux naturels, mais dès l'instant où vous coupez un arbre et l'utilisez pour construire, il a cessé de vivre, il ne pousse plus, il est inerte. Les matériaux que nous utilisons dans la construction ne sont pas naturels, ils ne changent pas au rythme des saisons ni des journées. Ce que nous créons est statique dans sa substance matérielle. Il est donc un contrepoint à la nature. Tout autour de nous, la nature est en perpétuel changement et l'architecture devrait contribuer à refléter ces changements. Je crois que cela nous permettrait d'intensifier notre perception des couleurs changeantes de la nature, des couleurs change-antes du jour, plutôt que d'essayer de faire changer l'architecture. J'ai défini un langage des formes qu'on ne trouve pas, me semble-t-il, dans la na-ture. Il est très difficile, à mon avis, pour ne pas dire impossible, de créer des formes aussi par-faites que celles présentes dans la nature. La nature fait ça mieux que nous, mais ce que nous pouvons faire en revanche, c'est concevoir des formes qui, d'une manière, sont inter-dépendantes sans qu'elles soient peut-être inter-dépendantes dans la nature. C'est ce que j'essaie de faire, je crois. Je m'efforce de trouver une forme de cons-truction qui ait de la signification sur le plan humain et un lien avec l'idée du lieu.»[4]

Le *High Museum of Art* d'Atlanta en Géorgie (1980–1983; ill. p. 80–83) se présente comme la synthèse des thèmes de prédilection de l'architecte et des multiples influences qui ont joué un rôle dans l'évolution de son œuvre. Une longue rampe mène à l'entrée comme dans l'Atheneum, mais ici, le volume central, la «nef» de l'édifice, c'est le mo-numental atrium. Ayant travaillé sur la petite salle de lecture Aye Simon du musée Guggenheim (1977–1978), Meier a pu réfléchir à loisir sur les qualités et les faiblesses des concepts architectu-raux de Wright. «J'ai beaucoup appris du Guggen-heim», raconte-t-il, «vous voyez une œuvre, mais si vous vous placez de l'autre côté de la rampe et la regardez à travers l'espace, elle vous apparaît sous un tout autre jour.» Au High Museum, Meier a multiplié les points de vue sur les œuvres d'art exposées, mais il a su aussi éviter les problèmes causés par la galerie en spirale de Wright en sépa-rant les rampes de circulation des galeries d'expo-sition. «Dans une certaine mesure, l'atrium inondé de lumière s'inspire de – ou commente – l'espace central du musée Guggenheim» conclut Meier.

Aye Simon Reading Room, Solomon R. Guggenheim Museum, New York, 1977–1978

Aye-Simon-Lesesaal, Solomon R. Guggenheim Museum, New York, 1977–1978

Salle de lecture Aye Simon, Solomon R. Guggenheim Museum, New York, 1977–1978

The Challenge of Europe

Meier's sense of order remains a prominent feature of the projects he undertook in Europe beginning in the late 1970s. It would seem, though, that the richness of the architectural environment of the Old Continent inspired him in new ways, and obliged him to address the issue of the context of his architecture more than in his earlier work. The first significant example of this trend is the *Museum for the Decorative Arts* which he built along the banks of the Main in Frankfurt (1979–1985; ill. pp. 68–75). The site is situated on the Museumsufer, on the bank of the river opposite the modern downtown area, and includes the 19th century Villa Metzler. Using the vocabulary which had by now become a trademark, Richard Meier chose to enter into a close dialogue with this bourgeois house, to surprisingly successful effect. He uses the cubic volume of the Villa to determine the 17,6 meter width and height of each quadrant of his grid. Rotating part of the museum structure by 3,5°, he emphasizes the alignment of the river embankment as opposed to that of the original house. An internal ramp and numerous openings permit a constant evolution of the points of view of the visitor, along the lines of High Museum, but without the central atrium. As though to prove that his buildings are more than isolated jewels, he links the Villa Metzler to the new museum via a glass bridge, making quite a natural connection, despite the radical difference in styles. Finally, the omnipresent white of his architecture here becomes an echo of the past which is far removed from Le Corbusier's purism. Rather it brings to mind the very German Baroque churches which he had gone to visit from Rome in 1973, when he said, "There is a sense of the spiritual in the use of light in all of the great Baroque churches. There, light is central to the experience of the architectural volume; certainly I have used light to a similar end." As always, confirming the wide range of his indirect sources, Richard Meier also commented that the use of light in the Frankfurt Museum "is not in the style of Louis Kahn, but it is in his spirit." Few 20th century architects have mastered light and space as well as the author of the Salk Institute (La Jolla, California, 1959–1965), or the Kimbell Art Museum (Fort Worth, Texas, 1966–1972), and Meier's homage to him is particularly interesting with respect to frequent statements that the New York Five strongly opposed Kahn's "Beaux-Arts modernity."

Before the opening of the Frankfurt Museum, Richard Meier was quite happy to have journalists visit the empty building, as though to signal that

Wie hier erwecken Meiers Bauten häufig den Anschein uneinnehmbarer Bastionen der Perfektion, die sich von ihrer Umgebung isolieren. Seine lichtüberfluteten Volumen wirken zwar nicht unbedingt steril, setzen sich aber mit ihrer Perfektion und ihrer weißen Farbe deutlich von der Unordnung des Lebens ab. Richard Meier sagt: »Ich glaube, der Architekt hat die Aufgabe, ein Gefühl der Ordnung zu schaffen, ein Gefühl des Ortes, ein Gefühl der Beziehungen. Diese Ideen sind Teil der Architektur, und deshalb sind Präzision oder Beziehungen sehr wichtig für mich, denn sie machen alles so klar wie möglich und schaffen ein Gefühl der Ordnung. Ich bin nicht daran interessiert, Chaos herzustellen, das können andere machen.«

Die Herausforderung Europas

Meiers Sinn für Ordnung blieb auch in den Projekten, die er in den späten siebziger Jahren in Europa in Angriff nahm, ein beherrschendes Merkmal. Doch der architektonische Reichtum des Alten Kontinents inspirierte ihn zugleich auf neue Weise und zwang ihn, den Kontext seiner Bauten mehr als früher einzubeziehen. Das erste signifikante Beispiel dafür ist das *Museum für Kunsthandwerk* in Frankfurt am Main (1979–1985; Abb. S. 68–75). Es liegt am Museumsufer gegenüber dem Stadtzentrum und schließt die Villa Metzler aus dem 19. Jahrhundert ein. Meier benutzte das Vokabular, das sein Markenzeichen geworden war, und ließ sich mit überraschendem Erfolg auf einen engen Dialog mit diesem großbürgerlichen Haus ein. Er benutzte den kubischen Baukörper der Villa, um die 17,60 m Seitenlänge seines quadratischen Rasters festzulegen. Durch die Verschwenkung des Museumsbaus um 3,5° betonte er den Verlauf des Flusses im Gegensatz zur Lage des bestehenden Hauses. Eine innere Rampe und zahlreiche Öffnungen bieten dem Besucher immer neue Blickpunkte, ähnlich wie beim High Museum, aber ohne das zentrale Atrium. Als müsse er beweisen, daß seine Bauten mehr sind als isolierte Pretiosen, verknüpfte er die Villa Metzler durch eine Glasbrücke mit dem neuen Museum, so daß trotz der radikalen Stilunterschiede eine natürliche Verbindung entstand. Das allgegenwärtige Weiß seiner Architektur wird hier zum Echo einer Vergangenheit, die weit von Le Corbusiers Purismus entfernt ist. Es erinnert eher an die sehr deutschen Barockkirchen, die er 1973 von Rom aus besucht hatte. Damals sagte er: »Bei all den großen Barockkirchen liegt eine gewisse Spiritualität in der Verwendung des Lichts. Dort spielt das Licht eine zentrale Rolle für die Erfahrung des architektonischen Volu-

Small silver bowl, designed by Richard Meier for Swid Powell in 1985

Kleine Silberschale, von Richard Meier für Swid Powell entworfen, 1985

Petite coupe en argent, dessinée par Richard Meier pour Swid Powell en 1985

Développant son répertoire de volumes curvilignes et rectilignes déjà visible dans des projets
antérieurs, l'architecte définit l'atrium du High
Museum comme un lieu de réunion ou un centre
culturel pour cette ville du Sud. La notion de ras-
semblement implique cependant l'idée d'un édifice
centré sur lui-même. La rampe de circulation est
une invitation lancée aux passants, mais toute
réunion ne peut se produire qu'au cœur de l'édifice. Les constructions de Meier sont souvent
apparues comme les bastions inviolables de la perfection, détachées de leur environnement. Bien
qu'il soit difficile de sous-entendre que ses volumes illuminés projettent une image de stérilité,
leur perfection, c'est-à-dire leur blancheur immaculée, semble en faire des objets fort éloignés du
désordre de l'existence. «La tâche de l'architecte»,
dit Richard Meier, «est de créer un sens de l'ordre,
un sens du lieu, un sens des rapports. Ces notions
sont bien entendu inhérentes à l'architecture, mais
la précision – ou les rapports – me semble très
importante dans la mesure où elle rend les idées
ou les rapports aussi clairs que possible et crée un
certain sens de l'ordre. Je n'ai pas envie de créer
du chaos, d'autres peuvent le faire à ma place.»

Le défi européen

Les projets européens sur lesquels l'architecte
travaille à partir de la fin des années soixante-dix se
caractérisent par ce sens de l'ordre. On a l'impression cependant que grâce à la richesse du cadre
architectural du Vieux Continent son inspiration se
soit renouvelée. Il semble avoir aussi abordé la
question du contexte de son architecture plus
sérieusement encore que dans ses réalisations
précédentes. Le premier exemple qui illustre cette
tendance est le *musée des Arts décoratifs* de
Francfort (1979–1985; ill. p. 68–75). Le site se
trouve sur la rive du Main, plus précisément sur le
Museumsufer, juste en face du quartier des
affaires. C'est à cet endroit aussi que fut édifiée au
XIXe siècle la villa Metzler. Reprenant ce fameux
vocabulaire devenu sa «marque de fabrique»,
Richard Meier choisit d'établir un dialo-gue avec la
maison de style bourgeois, démarche qui s'avère
étonnamment fructueuse. Il se sert du volume
cubique de la villa pour donner une unité de 17,6 m
aux carrés de la grille modulaire. En faisant pivoter
une partie de la structure sur un axe à 3,5°, il met
l'accent sur l'alignement du quai et l'oppose à celui
de la maison d'origine. Une rampe interne et une
multitude d'ouvertures assurent au visiteur une
superbe continuité visuelle comme au High
Museum, mais sans atrium central. Comme s'il

Louis Kahn: Central courtyard of the Salk Institute, La Jolla, California,
1959–1965

Louis Kahn: Zentraler Hof des Salk Institute, La Jolla, Kalifornien,
1959–1965

Louis Kahn: Espace central du Salk Institute, La Jolla, Californie,
1959–1965

Museum for the Decorative Arts, Frankfurt/Main, Germany, 1979–1985

Museum für Kunsthandwerk, Frankfurt am Main, Deutschland, 1979–1985

Musée des Arts décoratifs, Francfort-sur-le-Main, Allemagne, 1979–1985

the works of art to come might almost have been superfluous. A latent criticism of the museum is that it is indeed more powerful without its fill of German furniture and other objects. In a revealing comment, the architect said, "The project allowed me to make a work of art that forms a meaningful continuity with a broken cultural heritage." Referring to the departure of his own family from pre-war Germany, Richard Meier thus crosses the unspoken barrier which has long stood between modern architecture and art. Unapologetic, he declares, "I consider most of my buildings as works of art."[5]

As the definitions of the word "art" have become more and more complex, often including forms of expression which are far less intellectually and culturally demanding than architecture, the critic is tempted to agree with Meier's appraisal of his own work. In a different time and place, John Ruskin (1819–1900) said, "No person who is not a great sculptor or painter *can* be an architect. If he is not a sculptor or painter, he can only be a *builder*." Richard Meier's architecture as an art form may attain its purest expression in his private houses, which are free of some of the constraints which weigh on public projects. Two examples, built at opposite ends of the United States in the mid-1980s illustrate his approach.

Above and below: Ackerberg House, Malibu, California, 1984–1986

Oben und unten: Haus Ackerberg, Malibu, Kalifornien, 1984–1986

Ci-dessus et ci-dessous: maison Ackerberg, Malibu, Californie, 1984–1986

Two Houses

The *Ackerberg House* (Malibu, California, 1984–1986; ill. pp. 88–93) may not be the most successful of Meier's houses, but its situation, on the edge of the Pacific Coast Highway, shows how the architect dealt with the advantages and problems of the site. This heavily traveled road leaves only a narrow strip of land along the beach where an incredible variety of homes have been built, one next to the other. But the dust and commotion of the Highway give way, on the beach side, to an incredible vista of light and space. In a way, such a site was perfectly adopted to Meier's natural tendency to close one facade of his buildings while leaving the others open. From the roadside, the articulated white facade and glass blocks, usually viewed from a speeding car, only give a slight hint of what is within. There, after passing a guest wing, now being partially converted for the owner's use, the visitor enters a space of almost unlimited perspective, opening out onto the Pacific Ocean. Though offering privacy from neighbors, the Ackerberg House could hardly be more open, to nature, or indeed to art. The owners' substantial collection of contemporary art is given

mens. Sicherlich habe ich das Licht zu einem ähnlichen Zweck benutzt.« Ein Beweis für die Vielzahl seiner indirekten Quellen ist Meiers Kommentar zur Lichtführung in dem Frankfurter Museum, die »nicht im Stil Louis Kahns, aber in seinem Geiste ist«. Wenige Architekten des 20. Jahrhunderts haben Licht und Raum so meisterhaft beherrscht wie der Erbauer des Salk Institute (La Jolla, California, 1959–1965) oder des Kimbell Art Museum (Fort Worth, Texas, 1966–1972).

Vor der Eröffnung des Frankfurter Museums ließ Richard Meier die Journalisten gern das leere Gebäude inspizieren, als wolle er zu verstehen geben, daß die kommenden Kunstwerke beinahe überflüssig seien. Tatsächlich wird an dem Gebäude kritisiert, daß es ohne seine Sammlung deutscher Möbel und anderer Objekte mehr Ausdruckskraft besitzt. In einem enthüllenden Kommentar sagte der Architekt: »Das Projekt ermöglichte es mir, ein Kunstwerk zu schaffen, das eine sinnvolle Kontinuität zu einem unterbrochenen kulturellen Erbe herstellt.« Damit bezieht sich Meier auf den Fortgang seiner Familie aus dem Deutschland der Vorkriegszeit und überquert zugleich die unsichtbare Grenze, die lange Zeit moderne Architektur und Kunst trennte. Selbstbewußt verkündet er: »Ich betrachte die meisten meiner Bauten als Kunstwerke.«

Da die Definitionen des Wortes »Kunst« immer komplexer geworden sind und häufig Ausdrucksformen einschließen, die intellektuell und kulturell weitaus anspruchsloser sind als die Architektur, ist der Kritiker versucht, Meiers Einschätzung seines eigenen Werks zuzustimmen. Richard Meiers Architektur als Kunstform erreicht ihren vielleicht reinsten Ausdruck in seinen Privathäusern, denn sie sind frei von jenen Zwängen, die auf öffentlichen Projekten lasten. Zwei Bauten an den entgegengesetzten Enden der Vereinigten Staaten sind Beispiele dafür.

Zwei Häuser

Das *Haus Ackerberg* (Malibu, California, 1984–1986; Abb. S. 88–93), ist vielleicht nicht Meiers erfolgreichstes Wohnhaus, doch seine Lage am Pacific Coast Highway macht deutlich, wie der Architekt mit den Problemen und Vorzügen des Grundstücks umging. Der vielbefahrene Highway läßt nur einen schmalen Landstreifen entlang des Strandes frei, auf dem dicht nebeneinander unglaublich viele Häuser errichtet wurden. Doch Lärm und Schmutz des Highway weichen auf der Strandseite einem herrlichen Ausblick auf Licht und Raum. Ein solches Grundstück entsprach in mancher Hinsicht

voulait prouver que ses édifices sont plus que de beaux objets isolés, Meier lia la villa Metzler au nouveau musée par un pont en verre, créant une connexion naturelle entre les deux structures et ce, malgré leur grande différence de styles. Enfin, la présence omniprésente du blanc dans cette construction est un écho du passé sans rapport avec le Purisme de Le Corbusier. Il est en effet la réminiscence des églises baroques allemandes que Meier a visitées pendant son séjour à Rome en 1973. Il dit à ce propos: «Il y a un sens du spirituel dans le traitement de la lumière dans toutes les grandes églises baroques. La lumière s'y révèle essentielle pour appréhender le volume architectural. J'ai utilisé la lumière dans un but similaire, assurément.» Richard Meier explique encore que le traitement de la lumière dans le musée de Francfort «n'est pas dans le style de Louis Kahn mais dans l'esprit de celui-ci», confirmant par là la variété de ses sources d'inspiration, même indirectes. Peu d'architectes de ce siècle peuvent se vanter d'avoir maîtrisé la lumière et l'espace comme le père du Salk Institute (La Jolla, Californie, 1959–1965) ou du Kimbell Art Museum (Fort Worth, Texas, 1966–1972).

Avant l'ouverture officielle du musée de Francfort, Richard Meier fut heureux de faire visiter les salles vides à des journalistes comme s'il voulait montrer que les œuvres d'art à venir étaient presque superflues. Justement, une des critiques formulées à l'égard du musée est que vide il en impose plus que rempli de ses meubles allemands et autres objets exposés. L'architecte déclare de façon significative: «Le projet m'a permis de créer une œuvre d'art qui exprime la continuité retrouvée d'un patrimoine culturel brisé.» En faisant ainsi référence au départ de sa famille de l'Allemagne d'avant-guerre, Richard Meier franchit le fossé implicite qui a séparé pendant longtemps l'architecture moderne de l'art. Non sans assurance, il précise: «Je considère la plupart de mes constructions comme des œuvres d'art.»[5]

Comme l'art est devenu une notion d'une complexité croissante qui inclut souvent des formes d'expression beaucoup moins exigeantes sur le plan intellectuel et culturel que l'architecture, le critique est tenté d'approuver Meier dans l'appréciation qu'il donne de son propre travail. L'architecture de Meier en tant que forme d'art peut atteindre son expression la plus pure dans ses édifices privés, libérés en partie des contraintes pesant sur les projets publics. Deux exemples, pris aux deux extrémités des Etats-Unis et réalisés pendant la décennie quatre-vingt, illustrent ce propos.

Internationale Bauausstellung Housing, Berlin, Germany, 1982

Internationale Bauausstellung, Wohnbebauung, Berlin, Deutschland, 1982

Etude de logements pour l'exposition internationale des constructions, Berlin, Allemagne, 1982

Above and below: two views of the Grotta House, Harding Township, New Jersey, 1985–1989

Oben und unten: zwei Ansichten des Hauses Grotta, Harding Township, New Jersey, 1985–1989

Ci-dessus et ci-dessous: deux vues de la maison Grotta, Harding Township, New Jersey, 1985–1989

an ideal setting, where the colors and forms of the works engage in a dialogue with the architecture which has its parallels in the relation of the house to its natural setting. "As an artist or as an architect," says Meier, "one has a choice: representational art or abstract art. Abstraction allows architecture to express its own organizational and spatial consequences, it permits the creation of space without confusing its volume with any superimposed system of meaning or value." The responsive qualities of this house permit it to receive the colors of a painting by Sam Francis as well as the provocative sensuality of Robert Graham's sculptures of nude young women.

The *Grotta House* (Harding Township, New Jersey, 1985–1989; ill. p. 102–105) offers a very different set of qualities in terms of its site. A continent away from the architectural jumble of Los Angeles, this structure is located on a sloping three hectare plot of meadow land, surrounded only at a distance by neo-Colonial style farms. It may be that the purity of Richard Meier's buildings inspires some owners, but the Grottas must be considered almost ideal clients. A childhood friend of Meier's, Mr. Grotta chose the precise location of the house, on top of a gentle hill, with the architect. Well after the completion of the house, its owners insist that every detail be maintained in perfect condition, and stray objects seem to be banned from sight. Mr. Grotta's sense of the priority of the architecture made him go so far as to reject the idea of any kind of sun screen in the cylindrical living room area, preferring to deal with the summer heat rather than upset the purity of the forms. Undoubtedly applying the lessons learned in his museums, Richard Meier designed his sixteenth house to permit 360° viewing of the owners' unusual crafts collection. A curious detail is that an entry bridge which brings to mind earlier Meier houses is situated at the rear of the house, at the top of the hill, where a swimming pool had been planned. The actual entrance to the house is at the end of a covered walkway leading to the parking area. The sculptural door handles, repeated throughout the house, are inspired by the floor plan, a circle overlaid by a square, with the extending line of the walkway. Rigorous and relatively simple in its design, the Grotta House offers unexpected surfaces in a Meier building such as gray enamel paneling and large wall surfaces toward the kitchen and rear in ground-faced concrete block. Mr. Grotta marvels at the way this house lives in different types of light, from the rising sun to the brightness of a full moon. Within,

Meiers natürlicher Tendenz, eine Seite seiner Bauten zu schließen und die andere offenzulassen. Von der Straße her geben die gegliederte weiße Fassade und die Glasbausteine, gewöhnlich aus einem schnell fahrenden Auto gesehen, kaum einen Hinweis auf das Innere. Der Besucher geht an einem Gästeflügel vorbei, der heute teilweise vom Besitzer selbst genutzt wird, und betritt dann einen Bereich mit nahezu unbegrenztem Ausblick, der sich auf den Pazifischen Ozean öffnet. Obwohl das Haus Ackerberg den Nachbarn gegenüber abgeschirmt ist, könnte es der Natur oder auch der Kunst gegenüber kaum offener sein. Die beachtliche Kunstsammlung des Besitzers hat eine ideale Umgebung gefunden, in der Formen und Farben der Werke einen Dialog mit der Architektur führen, der in der Beziehung des Hauses zu seiner natürlichen Umgebung eine Parallele hat. »Als Künstler wie als Architekt steht man vor der Wahl: gegenständliche oder abstrakte Kunst«, sagt Meier. »Die Abstraktion erlaubt es der Architektur, ihre eigenen organisatorischen und räumlichen Konsequenzen zum Ausdruck zu bringen, sie ermöglicht die Schaffung von Raum, ohne daß ihr Volumen durch ein auferlegtes Bedeutungs- oder Wertesystem gestört würde.« Dank seiner Offenheit nimmt dieses Haus die Farben eines Bildes von Sam Francis ebenso auf wie die provokante Sinnlichkeit von Robert Grahams Skulpturen weiblicher Akte.

Das *Haus Grotta* (Harding Township, New Jersey, 1985–1989; Abb. S. 102–105) hat vom Grundstück her völlig andere Voraussetzungen. Es scheint einen Kontinent entfernt vom architektonischen Chaos der Stadt Los Angeles, auf einem abfallenden, drei Hektar großen Wiesengelände gelegen, das nur in der Ferne von Farmen im Neokolonialstil gesäumt ist. Wohl aufgrund der Lektionen, die er bei seinen Museen gelernt hatte, ermöglichte Meier bei diesem Haus, seinem sechzehnten, eine Rundumperspektive auf die ungewöhnliche Sammlung des Hausbesitzers. Kurioserweise liegt eine Eingangsbrücke, die an frühere Häuser Meiers erinnert, an der Rückseite des Hauses auf der Höhe des Hügels, wo ursprünglich ein Schwimmbecken geplant war. Der eigentliche Eingang befindet sich am Ende eines überdeckten Ganges, der zum Parkplatz führt. Die skulpturalen Türgriffe im ganzen Haus sind durch den Grundriß inspiriert, einen von einem Quadrat überlagerten Kreis, zu dem die Gerade des überdachten Ganges gehört. Das strenge und relativ einfache Haus Grotta bietet für einen Meier-Bau unerwartete Flächenbehandlungen wie etwa graue Emailplatten und große Wandflächen aus Betonstein an Küche und

Deux maisons

La première de ces résidences, la *maison Ackerberg* (Malibu, Californie, 1984–1986; ill. p. 88–93) n'est peut-être pas la plus réussie de toutes, mais son adaptation au site, au bord de la Pacific Coast Highway, montre très bien comment l'architecte a traité les avantages et les contraintes d'un tel emplacement. Cette route très fréquentée ne laisse qu'une étroite bande de terre le long de la plage où ont été construites de nombreuses maisons, hétéroclites et bigarrées. Mais, côté plage, le vacarme et la poussière font place à un grandiose panorama composé de lumière et d'espace. D'une certaine manière, un tel site convenait parfaitement à Meier qui, dans ses constructions, a une tendance naturelle à fermer la façade extérieure et à ouvrir l'autre. Côté route, la façade blanche et les briques de verre très bien articulées, qu'on voit habituellement d'une voiture lancée à grande vitesse, ne donnent qu'une vague idée de ce qu'il y a à l'intérieur de la maison. Après avoir dépassé l'aile des invités, réservée en partie aujourd'hui à l'usage du propriétaire, le visiteur pénètre dans un espace ouvert, avec une perspective presque illimitée sur l'immensité de l'océan Pacifique. Bien qu'offrant un espace privé, cette maison pourrait être difficilement plus ouverte à la nature, ou même à l'art. L'importante collection d'art contemporain des propriétaires y a trouvé un cadre idéal: une osmose s'est établie entre les couleurs et les formes des œuvres exposées et l'architecture environnante, osmose à mettre en parallèle avec le rapport de la maison au site naturel. «L'artiste ou l'architecte», dit Meier, «a le choix entre l'art figuratif et l'art abstrait. L'abstraction permet à l'architecture d'exprimer ses propres conséquences spatiales et organisationnelles, de créer un espace sans confondre son volume avec quelque système de valeurs ou de significations en surimpression. Grâce à sa réceptivité et à son dynamisme, cette maison peut accueillir aussi bien les couleurs d'un tableau de Sam Francis que la sensualité provocatrice des sculptures d'un Robert Graham représentant des jeunes femmes dénudées.

La seconde résidence, la *maison Grotta* (Harding Township, New Jersey, 1985–1989; ill. p. 102–105), présente des particularités fort différentes en ce qui concerne sa localisation. A l'autre bout du continent, loin du pêle-mêle architectural de Los Angeles, se trouve le site de cette construction: une prairie en pente douce d'une superficie de trois hectares, entourée d'assez loin par des fermes bâties dans le style néo-colonial du XVIIIe siècle. Fort des acquis que la construction de

Suspended canopy at the entrance of the Royal Dutch Paper Mills Headquarters (KNP-BT), Hilversum, The Netherlands, 1987–1992

Vordach der Hauptverwaltung Königlich Niederländische Papierfabrik (KNP-BT), Hilversum, Niederlande, 1987–1992

Marquise suspendue à l'entrée du siège des Papeteries Royales Néerlandaises (KNP-BT), Hilversum, Pays-Bas, 1987–1992

at night, continues the owner, the light of the moon, "silver and effervescent", is sufficient to define these volumes and make them shimmer.

Hilversum and The Hague

Perfection is also the byword in Richard Meier's first completed project in Holland, the Headquarters of the *Royal Dutch Paper Mills* (KNP-BT; Hilversum, The Netherlands, 1987–1992; ill. pp. 108–111). Located near Schiphol airport between Amsterdam and The Hague, Hilversum is a wealthy suburban neighborhood. An otherwise unmarked forest lane is the route into this unexpected site, although the building is visible from the nearby A27 highway. The two linked structures, a reception building and an 80 meter long, two-story office wing, elevated on pilotis to permit parking below, stand out against this green background with their complex, articulated white facades. Although 90 x 90 cm white aluminum panels are a prominent feature of the external cladding, there is also a subtle dividing wall of light beige Spanish limestone. Designed as a meeting place and office space for just 55 directors, the use of this building has varied somewhat with the March 1993 merger of KNP, a producer of graphic paper, board and packaging, with Bührmann-Tetterode and the VRG Group. KNP-BT is now a conglomerate of some 160 companies employing 28,000 people around the world. Criticized as being very "un-Dutch" by a local newspaper, perhaps because of the substantial means used for a relatively small building, the KNP-BT Headquarters does in fact make a bow to local architectural personalities such as William Marinus Dudok (1884–1974), who built the nearby town hall, or perhaps to Gerrit Rietveld, whose Schröder House in Utrecht (1924), or Erasmuslaan apartment house in the same neighboring city (1930–1935), seem to have influenced Meier here. When asked about this similarity, the architect responded, "You can't ignore things that you have seen in the past, that have impressed you, or extraordinary works of architecture. To say that there is direct reference would be wrong, but I wanted to have some of the tautness of Dutch architecture. It's a reference to many architects, but it's not intended as a direct reference to anyone."

Although the KNP-BT building does have many qualities, it may be criticized on the grounds of its formal complexity, especially in the numerous geometric details, which seem to exist to prove that this architect is a virtuoso. This Meier building, like some others, seems quite simply to have a bit too

Rückseite. Grotta ist begeistert davon, wie er in diesem Haus die unterschiedlichen Lichtverhältnisse erlebt, von der aufgehenden Sonne bis zur Helle einer Vollmondnacht. Nachts reicht im Inneren das Licht des Mondes, »silbern und schäumend«, wie der Besitzer sagt, um diese Volumen zu definieren und in Glanz zu hüllen.

Hilversum und Den Haag

Perfektion ist auch das Schlüsselwort für Richard Meiers erstes Gebäude in Holland, die Hauptverwaltung der *Königlich Niederländischen Papierfabrik* (KNP-BT; Hilversum, Niederlande, 1987–1992; Abb. S. 108–111).

Hilversum liegt nahe dem Flughafen Schiphol zwischen Amsterdam und Den Haag und ist eine wohlhabende Kleinstadt. Die beiden miteinander verbundenen Gebäudeteile, ein Empfangsgebäude und ein 80 m langer, zweigeschossiger Büroflügel, der sich auf Pilotis erhebt, damit darunter Autos parken können, bilden mit ihren gegliederten weißen Fassaden einen Kontrast zu dem grünen Hintergrund. Obwohl die Außenverkleidung von den 90 x 90 cm großen weißen Aluminiumplatten beherrscht wird, gibt es auch eine subtile Trennwand aus hellbeigem Kalkstein. Ursprünglich war das Gebäude als Versammlungsort und Bürobereich für nur 55 Direktoren bestimmt, doch die Nutzung änderte sich, als im März 1993 die KNP, die Zeichenpapier, Karton und Verpackungen herstellte, mit Bührmann-Tetterode und der VRG-Gruppe fusionierte. Eine Lokalzeitung kritisierte die Hauptverwaltung als sehr »unholländisch«, vielleicht, weil für ein relativ kleines Gebäude beträchtliche Mittel ausgegeben wurden. Dabei entrichtet die KNP-BT örtlichen Architekten einen Tribut, etwa an William Marinus Dudok (1884–1974), der das nahegelegene Rathaus errichtete, oder vielleicht auch an Gerrit Rietveld, dessen Haus Schröder in Utrecht (1924) oder Mietshaus am Erasmuslaan in derselben Nachbarstadt (1930–1935) Meier hier beeinflußt haben könnten. Als man ihn nach dieser Verwandtschaft fragte, erwiderte Meier: »Man kann Dinge nicht ignorieren, die man in der Vergangenheit gesehen hat, die einen beeindruckt haben, oder außergewöhnliche Werke der Architektur. Es wäre falsch zu sagen, daß es einen direkten Bezug gibt, aber ich wollte etwas von der Straffheit der holländischen Architektur haben. Es hat Bezüge zu vielen Architekten, aber es ist nicht als direkter Bezug auf irgend jemanden gedacht.«

Obwohl das KNP-BT-Gebäude viele Qualitäten besitzt, ließe es sich wegen seiner formalen Kom-

musées lui avait donnés, Richard Meier dessina sa seizième maison de manière à assurer une visibilité à 360° de la belle collection d'art populaire des propriétaires. Détail curieux, une passerelle qui rappelle les premières constructions de Meier est située à l'arrière de la maison, au sommet de la colline, à l'endroit où une piscine avait été prévue. La vraie entrée se trouve au bout d'un passage piétonnier couvert conduisant à l'aire de parking. Les poignées de portes sculpturales, thème récurrent de la maison, s'inspirent de la géométrie du plan, un cercle superposé d'un carré, avec la ligne de prolongement du passage. La Grotta House, d'un dessin rigoureux et plutôt simple, présente des surfaces inattendues pour une construction de Meier telles que les panneaux émaillés de couleur grise ou les grandes surfaces murales du côté de la cuisine ou de l'arrière de la maison en parpaings de béton rugueux.

Hilversum et La Haye
Le premier projet réalisé par Meier aux Pays-Bas, des bureaux pour le Papeteries Royales Néerlandaises (KNP-BT; Hilversum, Pays-Bas, 1987–1992; ill. p. 108–111), est lui aussi l'image même de la perfection. Située près de l'aéroport de Schiphol, entre Amsterdam et La Haye, Hilversum est une commune suburbaine aisée. Le complexe se compose de deux structures reliées entre elles, un bâtiment pour la réception et une aile de 80 m de long pour les bureaux, constituée de deux étages sur pilotis avec une aire de parking en dessous. Avec ses façades blanches bien articulées, l'édifice se détache sur le fond vert de la forêt. Si des panneaux en aluminium de couleur blanche mesurant 90 cm de côté constituent le composant essentiel de l'habillage extérieur, il y a aussi un beau mur mitoyen en calcaire d'Espagne beige clair. Prévu au départ comme lieu de réunion et espace de bureaux pour quelque cinquante-cinq dirigeants de l'entreprise, l'usage de ce complexe a légèrement varié depuis la fusion en mars 1993 de KNP, producteur de papier graphique, cartonnage et emballage, avec Bührmann-Tetterode et le groupe VRG. L'immeuble de KNP-BT, critiqué par un journal local comme étant «non-hollandais», peut-être à cause des moyens financiers importants utilisés pour un édifice relativement petit, est en réalité une révérence faite à des architectes originaires de la région comme William Marinus Dudok (1884–1974) qui construisit l'hôtel de ville tout proche, ou peut-être Gerrit Rietveld dont la maison Schröder (1924) et le bâtiment sur Erasmuslaan (1930–1935) dans la ville d'Utrecht

Gerrit Rietveld/Truus Schröder: Schröder House, Utrecht, The Netherlands, 1924

Gerrit Rietveld/Truus Schröder: Haus Schröder, Utrecht, Niederlande, 1924

Gerrit Rietveld/Truus Schröder: maison Schröder, Utrecht, Pays-Bas, 1924

Entrance facade of the Royal Dutch Paper Mills, Headquarters, Hilversum, The Netherlands, 1987–1992

Eingangsfassade der Hauptverwaltung Königlich Niederländische Papierfabrik, Hilversum, Niederlande, 1987–1992

Façade des Papeteries Royales Néerlandaises, Hilversum, Pays-Bas, 1987–1992

much architecture. The point, that Richard Meier is capable of extraordinary combinations of geometry, could have been made with less fussy attention to detail, but then, as he has said, "Architecture is the subject of my architecture."

The KNP-BT commission was awarded to Richard Meier without a competition one year after he was selected to build the new *Hague City Hall* (1986–1995; ill. pp. 112–115). The result of a limited competition in which architects were coupled with contractors, the project to build a new municipal building on this site had been considered for 80 years. Close to the modern Centraal train station, this section of The Hague houses numerous governmental offices, such as the neighboring Ministry of Justice. The final decision to build a large, open city hall, together with a public library here, was related to the realization that an area given over entirely to offices during the day becomes devoid of life at night. It is in fact a final major element of the so-called "Culture Square" project, which includes the nearby theaters designed by the architects Herman Hertzberger and Rem Koolhaas. Adjacent to this group of buildings, the developer MAB is undertaking the construction of a large project known as "The Resident", which is intended to include 100,000 m² of office space, 4,600 m² of shops, 380 apartments and 790 parking places. Subsequent to the appointment of Rob Krier as the "urban specialist" for the area in 1988, Cesar Pelli was chosen to build a 20-story corporate headquarters for the Zurich Insurance Company, and Michael Graves to re-design a 1960s building for the Dutch Ministry of Culture. Ominously, this second project is called "The Transitorium."

All of this background gives some idea of the dense urban area of the new City Hall, located on a wedge-shaped site between the pedestrian Turf-markt, Kalvermarkt, and the busier, more commercial Spui. The site, like most of the center of the city, belongs to the Dutch government, but it is being developed by the ABP Pension Fund, on the basis of a long-term lease. Clad inside and out with 85 x 180 cm porcelain-enameled metal panels, the structure has twelve and ten story office blocks which diverge from each other by 12,5°, underlining the rotation of the city's own grids, and creating a triangular internal volume. It is here that Meier has placed what will be the biggest atrium in Europe, 47 meters high and as large as the Saint Mark's Place in Venice. Within, between banks of white-painted steel suspension bridges, there is the rounded volume of the City Council chambers, and

plexität kritisieren, vor allem bei den zahlreichen geometrischen Details, die offenbar demonstrieren sollen, daß dieser Architekt ein Virtuose ist. Wie manche anderen Bauten Meiers zeigt die Hauptverwaltung einfach ein wenig zu viel Architektur. Daß Richard Meier höchst ungewöhnliche geometrische Kombinationen herzustellen vermag, hätte auch mit einer weniger hektischen Detaillierung bewiesen werden können. Doch wie Meier sagt: »Architektur ist das Thema meiner Architektur.«

Den Auftrag von KNP-BT erhielt Meier ohne Wettbewerb ein Jahr, nachdem er aus einem begrenzten Wettbewerb für das neue *Rathaus* in Den Haag (1986–1995; Abb. S. 112–115), bei dem Architekten mit Bauunternehmern zusammenarbeiteten, als Sieger hervorgegangen war. Die Idee, auf diesem Grundstück ein neues städtisches Gebäude zu errichten, war schon seit achtzig Jahren erwogen worden. Dieses Viertel Den Haags liegt in der Nähe des modernen Hauptbahnhofs und beherbergt zahlreiche Regierungsgebäude wie das benachbarte Justizministerium. Der Entschluß, das große, offene Rathaus mit einer öffentlichen Bibliothek zu verbinden, entstand aus der Erkenntnis, daß ein Bereich, der tagsüber nur von Büros besetzt ist, abends und nachts völlig ausgestorben wirkt. Zudem ist der Komplex ein wichtiges abschließendes Element des sogenannten »Kulturplatzes«, zu dem auch die nahegelegenen Theater der Architekten Herman Hertzberger und Rem Koolhaas gehören.

Vor diesem Hintergrund ist die Dichte der urbanen Struktur in der Umgebung des neuen Rathauses zu erkennen. Es liegt auf einem keilförmigen Grundstück zwischen der Fußgängerzone Turfmarkt und Kalvermarkt und dem lebhafteren, kommerzielleren Spui. Wie der größte Teil der Innenstadt gehört das Grundstück dem holländischen Staat, wird aber auf der Basis einer langfristigen Pacht von dem ABP-Pensionsfonds erschlossen. Der Komplex ist innen und außen mit 85 x 180 cm großen porzellan-emaillierten Metallplatten verkleidet. Er besteht aus zwölf und zehn Geschosse hohen Büroblocks, die um 12,5° gegeneinander verschwenkt sind, um die Rotation des Stadtrasters zu betonen. Dadurch ergibt sich ein nahezu dreieckiger Innenraum, in dem Meier das größte Atrium Europas unterbringen wird, 47 m hoch und so groß wie der Markusplatz in Venedig. Zwischen Reihen weißgestrichener Stahlbrücken liegen das gerundete Volumen des Ratssaals und ein Hochzeitssaal sowie die anderen notwendigen städtischen Einrichtungen. Dieser spektakuläre offene Raum könnte zu einer von Meiers berühm-

semblent avoir inspiré Meier. Lorsqu'on lui parle de ressemblance, l'architecte répond: «Vous ne pouvez ignorer les choses que vous avez vues dans le passé, qui vous ont impressionné ou les ouvrages d'architecture remarquables. Je souhaitais avoir un peu de la tension qui caractérise l'architecture hollandaise. C'est une référence à plusieurs architectes mais elle ne se veut pas une référence directe à l'un d'entre eux.»

En dépit des qualités évidentes de l'édifice de KNP-BT, on peut en critiquer la complexité formelle, en particulier le grand nombre de détails géométriques dont la seule justification serait de montrer la virtuosité du maître. Cette construction comme quelques autres œuvres de Meier donne l'impression d'avoir tout simplement un peu trop d'architecture. Que Richard Meier soit capable de combinaisons de géométries extraordinaires aurait pu être démontré avec moins de soin tatillon pour les détails, mais n'a-t-il pas dit lui-même «l'architecture est le sujet de mon architecture»?

Richard Meier reçoit la commande de KNP-BT, sans concours, un an après avoir été sélectionné pour construire le nouvel *hôtel de ville de La Haye* (1986–1995; ill. p. 112–115). Fruit d'une consultation au cours de laquelle des architectes furent associés à des entrepreneurs, le projet de bâtir une nouvelle administration municipale sur le site en question était déjà à l'étude depuis quatrevingts ans. Situé près de la gare Centraal, ce quartier de La Haye abrite de nombreux édifices gouvernementaux tels que le ministère de la Justice. Il fut décidé finalement de construire non seulement la grande mairie prévue depuis longtemps mais aussi une bibliothèque municipale: on avait pris conscience en effet qu'un quartier de bureaux très animé le jour était désespérément vide la nuit. Cette préoccupation joue un rôle essentiel dans le projet baptisé «Carré culturel», qui inclut les théâtres voisins dessinés par les architectes Herman Hertzberger et Rem Koolhaas.

Toutes ces précisions donnent une idée de la densité urbaine du site qui se trouve à l'angle de la zone piétonne du Turfmarkt, du Kalvermarkt et du Spui, plus animé et plus commerçant. Le site, comme la majeure partie du centre ville, est la propriété du gouvernement néerlandais, mais ce sont les assurances vieillesse ABP qui procèdent à son aménagement sur la base d'un bail à long terme. L'habillage extérieur et intérieur est constitué de panneaux en métal émaillé blanc de format 85 x 180 cm. La structure est divisée en deux immeubles de bureaux de douze et dix étages dont l'écartement correspond à un angle de 12,5°, sou-

Southeast elevation of The Hague City Hall and Central Library, The Hague, The Netherlands, 1986–1995, model

Südostfassade des Rathauses und der Zentralbibliothek, Den Haag, Niederlande, 1986–1995, Modell

Elévation sud-ouest de l'hôtel de ville de La Haye et de la librairie centrale, La Haye, Pays-Bas, 1986–1995, maquette

a wedding hall, together with the other necessary municipal facilities. This spectacular, open space should become one of Richard Meier's most famous architectural accomplishments, and it does in many ways symbolize his transition from a more intimate scale to the very large commissions which in fact are rarely given to architects of great talent. It is also symbolic of his growing awareness of the urban fabric, especially in the rich context of European cities, because it responds to a difficult architectural environment and offers numerous openings and points of passage.

Given the size of this project and the numerous decision-makers involved, it was probably inevitable that certain compromises would be forced on the architect. One of these is the presence, on the Spui side, of a merchant who had a previous claim to part of the site. While the neighboring library was still very much under construction, this dealer in inexpensive furniture had already installed his boutique. Despite the signature curved glass wall of the space, no amount of exterior design could quite erase the curious impression created by this shop situated on the axis of the main entrance to the atrium.

On the banks of the Seine

Although three times larger than his Canal+ building in Paris, The Hague City Hall was built with the same total budget, which is to say that Meier has had to innovate in order to create a new standard for inexpensive office buildings. Contrary to what might be expected, The Hague City Hall is one of the first Meier buildings to be designed on computers. Given the complexity and scale of the project, this proved to be an essential element in controlling costs.

Bianco Sardo granite was used on the floors of public spaces, but the building includes many prefabricated elements, and its painted concrete columns do not radiate the kind of quality one is accustomed to in a Meier building. If this is the price to pay in order to have a design of quality as opposed to the banal fare seen in most public buildings, then so be it. While adhering to a limited budget, Richard Meier has not compromised his architectural ideals, proving that good design can be afforded by a municipal government.

Designing for large corporations can undoubtedly be as frustrating for an architect as a municipal commission, but Richard Meier's international reputation, reinforced by his 1984 Pritzker Prize, and the Royal Gold Medal which he received in 1989, has been such that he has often been able to

testen Leistungen werden. In mancher Hinsicht symbolisiert er den Übergang des Architekten von einem intimeren Maßstab zu den sehr großen Aufträgen, die hochtalentierten Architekten im Grunde nur selten beschieden sind. Das Atrium ist auch ein Symbol seines zunehmenden Verständnisses für städtische Strukturen, vor allem im reichen Kontext europäischer Städte, denn es geht auf eine schwierige architektonische Umgebung ein und bietet zahlreiche Öffnungen und Passagen.

Angesichts der Größe dieses Projekts und der vielen Entscheidungsträger war es vielleicht unvermeidlich, daß der Architekt Kompromisse eingehen mußte. Dazu gehört zum Beispiel die Präsenz eines Kaufmanns an der Spui-Seite, der einen früheren Anspruch auf einen Teil des Grundstücks besaß. Während die angrenzende Bibliothek noch weitgehend im Bau war, hatte dieser Händler für billige Möbel bereits seinen Laden eröffnet. Trotz der charakteristischen gekurvten Glaswand kann kein noch so aufwendiges Design den merkwürdigen Eindruck verwischen, den dieses Geschäft auf der Achse des Haupteingangs zum Atrium hinterläßt.

Am Ufer der Seine

Obwohl dreimal größer als sein Canal+ Gebäude in Paris, wurde das Den Haager Rathaus mit dem gleichen Budget errichtet. Das bedeutet, daß Meier innovative Lösungen finden mußte, um einen neuen Standard für kostensparende Bürobauten zu schaffen. Überraschenderweise ist das Rathaus in Den Haag einer der ersten Bauten Meiers, die an Computern entworfen wurden. Angesichts der Komplexität und der Größe des Projekts erwies sich dieses Verfahren als wichtiger kostensenkender Faktor.

In den öffentlichen Bereichen des Rathauses wurde Bianco-Sardo-Granit für die Böden verwendet. Doch das Gebäude enthält auch viele präfabrizierte Elemente, und die gestrichenen Betonstützen demonstrieren nicht jenes Qualitätsbewußtsein, an das man bei einem Meier-Bau gewöhnt ist. Wenn dies der Preis ist, den man bezahlen muß, um einen exzellenten Bau zu erhalten, im Gegensatz zu der banalen Hausmannskost, die sonst bei den meisten öffentlichen Bauten anzutreffen ist, dann soll es so sein. Richard Meier hat jedenfalls, als er sich auf das begrenzte Budget einstellte, seine architektonischen Ideale nicht verraten und bewiesen, daß auch eine Stadtverwaltung sich gute Architektur leisten kann.

Entwürfe für große Firmen können für einen Architekten sicherlich ebenso frustrierend sein wie

lignant ainsi la rotation des deux grilles de la ville et créant un volume triangulaire interne. C'est à cet endroit précis que Meier a placé le plus grand atrium d'Europe d'une hauteur de 47 m et aussi vaste que la place Saint-Marc à Venise. A l'intérieur, entre les rangées de ponts suspendus en acier laqué blanc, se trouvent le volume rond de la grande salle de réunion du conseil municipal, la salle des mariages et les autres services municipaux. Cet espace ouvert, spectaculaire, devrait devenir l'une des réalisations architecturales les plus célèbres de Meier. A maints égards aussi, il symbolise dans son architecture la transition réussie des projets d'échelle modeste aux grandes commandes, qui sont rarement attribuées à des architectes de grand talent. Cette réalisation est également symbolique de sa prise de conscience grandissante de l'urbain, en particulier dans le contexte riche des villes européennes: elle est en effet une réponse à un environnement architectural lourd de complexité et offre force points d'ouverture et de passage.

Vu l'ampleur du projet et le nombre élevé de décideurs intervenant dans l'affaire, il était inévitable que l'architecte se voie imposer certains compromis. Le premier d'entre eux était la présence, du côté du Spui, d'un magasin dont le propriétaire jouissait d'un droit antérieur sur une partie du site. Alors que la bibliothèque était encore en construction, le marchand de meubles bon marché avait déjà terminé l'aménagement de sa boutique. Malgré la présence de l'immense verrière courbe – une des «signatures» de Meier – aucun dessin de façade ne put effacer la curieuse impression que ce magasin situé dans l'axe de l'entrée principale donnait à l'ensemble.

Sur les rives de la Seine
Bien que trois fois plus grand que l'immeuble de Canal+, l'hôtel de ville de La Haye a été construit dans une enveloppe financière identique.

Contrairement à ce qu'on pourrait penser, l'hôtel de ville est une des premières constructions de Meier à avoir été conçue par ordinateur. Etant donné la complexité et l'échelle du projet, c'était un moyen indispensable pour maîtriser les coûts.

On utilisa du granite bianco sardo pour les sols des espaces publics, mais de très nombreux éléments préfabriqués sont également présents dans la structure, sans oublier les colonnes en béton peintes qui ne dégagent pas la même qualité que celle à laquelle Meier nous a habitués. Si c'est le prix à payer pour avoir un dessin de qualité qui soit aux antipodes de l'affligeante banalité de la plupart des édifices publics, alors, acceptons-le. Bien que

View from a terrace of the Canal+ Headquarters Building, Paris, France, 1988–1992

Blick von einer Terrasse der Hauptverwaltung Canal+, Paris, Frankreich, 1988–1992

Vue d'une terrasse de Canal+, Paris, France, 1988–1992

work in privileged circumstances. This was in many ways the case for his *Canal+ Headquarters* building in Paris (1988 1992; ill. pp. 122 129). One of the most profitable private cable television companies in the world, Canal+ under the leadership of André Rousselet wanted to make an architectural "statement" with its new building, and Richard Meier seemed the logical choice for a forward-looking design. In 1981, Meier had already designed an unbuilt office complex for the auto-mobile manufacturer Renault, destined for a site not far from the Quai André-Citroën where the Canal+ building was erected. Built in a very short time span, between April 1990 and the end of 1991, this building is not blessed with a very good site, set back from the Left Bank of the Seine, near a good deal of mediocre modern architecture and relatively distant from the historic city-center. The only positive element in the immediate vicinity is the recently opened Parc Citroën. And yet Richard Meier has said, "I like to think of this building as Parisian in feeling, intellectual yet sensual, and beautiful in its rationality. Spatially it is simple, but technically it is complex. The building's sheer wall becomes the placard both for Canal+ and its urban presence. Its image from the Seine is of a great ship whose only movement is the changing light."

The plan of this new Richard Meier ship is in fact an "L", with production and office facilities clearly divided. As in other buildings, such as KNP-BT, the differing functions of Richard Meier's buildings often find an expression in the architectural form, running the risk, as seems to be the case here, of creating or reinforcing internal divisions among the personnel. When asked about this problem, Meier responds with some hesitation, "That's possible. I thought that we had solved the problem with the bridges and the atrium, and in the way in which you have to go from one side to another even to have lunch, so that there are places to come together and there are places to be separate, but it may be that there is... It's an issue I haven't heard before, but it's possible." In more general terms, why does he feel that the architecture should reflect the existence of different depart-ments or activities in a firm? "It's not so much dif-ferent departments. There are very different kinds of spaces, the studio spaces and the production spaces have totally different kinds of requirements in terms of light, space, scale, than the office spaces, so it seemed appropriate to have that expression."[6]

Undoubtedly one of the most striking and suc-cessful contemporary buildings built in Paris in a

Aufträge einer Stadtverwaltung. Doch Richard Meiers internationales Ansehen, verstärkt durch den Pritzker-Preis von 1984 und die Royal Gold Medal, die er 1989 erhielt, ist so groß, daß er häu-fig unter privilegierten Umständen arbeiten konnte. Das gilt zum Beispiel für die *Canal+ Hauptver-waltung* in Paris (1988–1992; Abb. S. 122–129). Canal+, eine der profitabelsten privaten Kabelfern-sehgesellschaften der Welt, wollte unter der Füh-rung André Rousselets aus seinem Gebäude ein architektonisches «Statement» machen. Richard Meier schien die logische Wahl für einen progres-siven Entwurf. Schon 1981 hatte Meier einen nicht realisierten Bürokomplex für den Automobilherstel-ler Renault entworfen, für ein Grundstück nahe jenes Quai André-Citroën, auf dem dann das Gebäude von Canal+ errichtet wurde. Die Haupt-verwaltung entstand in einem sehr kurzen Zeit-raum, zwischen April 1990 und Ende 1991. Das nicht sehr günstig geschnittene Grundstück liegt am linken Seineufer, von viel mittelmäßiger moder-ner Architektur umgeben und relativ weit vom historischen Stadtzentrum entfernt. Das einzige positive Element in der unmittelbaren Nachbar-schaft ist der jüngst eröffnete Parc Citroën. Den-noch sagte Richard Meier: »Ich denke mir dieses Gebäude gern als pariserisch, intellektuell und doch sinnlich, und schön in seiner Rationalität. Räumlich ist es einfach, aber technisch ist es kom-plex. Die glatte Wand des Gebäudes wird zum Plakat, für Canal+ und für seine urbane Präsenz. Von der Seine her sieht es aus wie ein großes Schiff, dessen einzige Bewegung im Wechsel des Lichts besteht.«

Der Grundriß dieses neuen Meier-Schiffs ist ein »L«, das Produktions-und Bürobereiche deutlich voneinander trennt. Wie bei anderen Bauten, etwa KNP-BT, drückt Meier unterschiedliche Funktionen häufig in der architektonischen Form aus. Dabei geht er das Risiko ein, wie es hier der Fall zu sein scheint, interne Abgrenzungen zwischen dem Personal zu schaffen oder zu verstärken. Auf die Frage nach diesem Problem antwortete Meier zö-gernd: »Das ist möglich. Ich dachte, wir hätten das Problem mit den Brücken und dem Atrium gelöst und damit, daß man sogar zum Essen von einer Seite zur anderen gehen muß, so daß es Orte zum Zusammenkommen und Orte zum Alleinsein gibt, aber vielleicht... Es ist ein Problem, von dem ich noch nicht gehört habe, aber es ist möglich.« Allgemeiner gefragt, warum glaubt er, daß die Architektur die Existenz verschiedener Abteilungen oder Aktivitäten in einer Firma reflektieren sollte? »Es geht nicht so sehr um verschiedene Abtei-

Entrance area of the Canal+ Headquarters Building, Paris, France, 1988–1992

Eingangsbereich der Canal+ Hauptverwaltung, Paris, Frankreich, 1988–1992

Espace d'entrée de Canal+, Paris, France, 1988–1992

le budget alloué ait été limité, Richard Meier n'a pas trahi ses idéaux architecturaux, prouvant ainsi qu'une belle architecture est à la portée d'une bourse municipale.

Concevoir un projet pour une grande compagnie peut s'avérer pour un architecte aussi frustrant qu'une commande publique, mais la renommée internationale de Richard Meier (consolidée par le prix Pritzker en 1988 et la Médaille d'Or Royale (RIBA) en 1989) était si bien établie qu'on lui offrit souvent l'occasion de travailler dans des conditions privilégiées. Ce fut le cas pour le *siège de Canal+* à Paris (1988–1992; ill. p. 122–129). A la direction de cette chaîne de télévision câblée, l'une des télévisions privées les plus rentables du monde, dont André Rousselet était le président, on désirait que les nouveaux locaux soient perçus comme une «profession de foi» architecturale. Il était donc logique qu'un architecte comme Richard Meier soit choisi pour concevoir une architecture ouverte sur l'avenir. En 1981 déjà, Meier avait conçu un projet d'immeuble administratif pour la Régie Renault. Ce projet, qui devait être réalisé non loin du Quai André-Citroën, où se trouve l'immeuble de Canal+, ne vit jamais le jour. Construit dans des délais très courts, entre avril 1990 et fin 1991, l'édifice de Canal+ n'est pas particulièrement gâté par le site: il se trouve sur la Rive gauche, un peu en retrait de la Seine, entouré de constructions modernes d'une grande médiocrité et assez éloigné du Paris historique. Le parc Citroën ouvert il y a peu de temps est le seul élément positif dans le voisinage. Pourtant Richard Meier dit: «J'aime à penser que cette construction est parisienne dans l'âme, intellectuelle mais sensuelle, belle aussi dans sa rationalité. Simple sur le plan spatial mais complexe sur le plan technique. Le mur de l'édifice devient à lui seul l'enseigne de Canal+ et de sa présence urbaine. Vu de la Seine, on dirait un grand bateau dont l'unique mouvement serait celui de la lumière changeante.»

Le plan de ce nouveau bateau de Meier correspond en fait à un «L», divisé clairement en une unité de production et une autre pour l'administration. La construction de lieux de travail à l'instar des Papeteries Royales Néerlandaises montre que chez Meier les différentes fonctions au sein de l'entreprise s'expriment souvent aussi dans la forme architecturale, ce qui fait courir le risque, comme cela semble être le cas ici, de créer ou de renforcer les divisions internes du personnel. Interrogé sur la question, Richard Meier répond après quelque hésitation: «C'est possible. Je pensais avoir résolu ce problème avec les ponts et

Aerial view of the model of the Renault Administrative Headquarters, Boulogne-Billancourt, France, 1981.

Luftansicht des Modells der Renault Hauptverwaltung, Boulogne-Billancourt, Frankreich, 1981.

Vue aérienne de la maquette du siège de Renault, Boulogne-Billancourt, France, 1981.

View through the "urban window" of the Canal+ Headquarters Building, Paris, France, 1988–1992

Blick durch das »Stadtfenster« der Canal+ Hauptverwaltung, Paris, Frankreich, 1988–1992

Vue à travers la «fenêtre urbaine» de Canal+, Paris, France, 1988–1992

number of years, the Canal+ Headquarters has two visible architectural features which give a sense of excitement to the building. One is the so-called "urban window," the large opening at the extremity of the facade facing the Seine. Although Richard Meier's architecture often plays on the rapport between the empty and the full, this empty frame intrigues and attracts both people who work in the building and those who see it from a distance. Another defining space is the glassed three-story entrance atrium, with its rough Vosges granite floors and its desk, also designed by Meier. From the first contact, visitors are given an image of architectural excitement and clarity, and these images are carried throughout the building, through such methods as the use of a particularly clear glass. This sort of material, like the granite, betrays the generous budget accorded by the client. Despite this facility, the Canal+ building remains a testimony to Meier's talent, not only because of the apparent design elements, but also because he had to face difficult zoning restrictions requiring varying heights, and other imposed factors such as the large studio and production spaces mentioned above, for which he provided only the external shell.

Back to Germany
During the later part of the 1980s, Richard Meier, like many other American architects received few commissions in the United States, aside of course from the enormous Getty Center. This was largely a question of economic circumstances. The recession though did not strike continental Europe as early as it did the United States, and after the Museum for the Decorative Arts, Frankfurt/Main, Meier's reputation in Germany was well established. Just two years after the Frankfurt building was completed, in 1986 he was awarded the daunting task of building on what the German press has called "one of the most problematic sites in the country," the Ulm Münsterplatz. A small city of 100,000, the birthplace of Albert Einstein, Ulm saw 85 % of its old section destroyed by bombing in 1944. Circumstances there after the war were such that no real effort was made to reconstitute the traditional architecture, as had been the case in Munich, for example. Rather, cheap, modern structures proliferated right up to the large square in front of the Ulm Minster, one monument which surprisingly escaped the Allied bombs all but un-scathed. At just over 160 meters in height, the single spire of the minster is the tallest of its kind, exceeding that of Cologne, which is a much larger

lungen. Es gibt sehr unterschiedliche Arten von Räumen, die Studioräume und die Produktionsräume haben in Licht, Größe, Maßstab völlig andere Anforderungen als die Büroräume, deshalb schien es angebracht, das zum Ausdruck zu bringen.«[6]

Die Canal+ Hauptverwaltung ist zweifellos einer der gelungensten und ungewöhnlichsten modernen Bauten, die in den letzten Jahren in Paris entstanden. Zwei besondere architektonische Merkmale verleihen dem Gebäude Dynamik. Das eine ist das sogenannte »Stadtfenster«, die große Öffnung am Ende der Fassade zur Seineseite. Obwohl Meiers Architektur häufig mit der Beziehung zwischen Leerem und Vollem spielt, wirkt dieser leere Rahmen irritierend und faszinierend; auf die Menschen, die im Inneren arbeiten ebenso wie auf jene, die ihn aus der Ferne sehen. Das zweite Charakteristikum ist das verglaste, drei Geschosse hohe Eingangsatrium mit seinem rauhen Fußboden aus Vogesengranit und dem von Meier entworfenen Pult. Vom ersten Augenblick an nehmen die Besucher ein Bild der architektonischen Klarheit und Dynamik auf, und diese Bilder sind überall im Gebäude fortgeführt, zum Beispiel durch die Verwendung eines speziellen Klarglases. Dieses Material verrät ebenso wie der Granit das großzügige Budget, das der Bauherr Meier gewährte. Dennoch bleibt Canal+ ein Zeugnis für das Talent des Architekten, nicht nur wegen der auffallenden Designelemente, sondern auch, weil er mit schwierigen Zonierungsbeschränkungen, die unterschiedliche Höhen erforderten, und anderen von außen auferlegten Faktoren konfrontiert war, wie etwa den großen Studio- und Produktionsbereichen, für die er nur die äußere Hülle schuf.

Wieder in Deutschland

Ende der achtziger Jahre erhielt Meier, wie viele andere amerikanische Architekten, nur wenige Aufträge in den Vereinigten Staaten, abgesehen natürlich von dem riesigen Getty Center. Ursache dafür waren in erster Linie die wirtschaftlichen Verhältnisse. Doch in Kontinentaleuropa trat die Rezession noch nicht so früh ein wie in Amerika, und Meier genoß seit dem Frankfurter Museum für Kunsthandwerk in Deutschland einen hervorragenden Ruf. Nur zwei Jahre nach der Vollendung des Museums in Frankfurt erhielt er 1986 die schwierige Aufgabe, an dem Ort zu bauen, den die deutsche Presse als den »problematischsten des Landes« bezeichnete, dem Ulmer Münsterplatz. In Ulm, einer Stadt mit 100 000 Einwohnern, dem Geburtsort Albert Einsteins, waren 85 % des alten

l'atrium et dans le système de circulation qui oblige à aller d'un point à un autre, même pour déjeuner, créant ainsi des lieux de rencontre et des lieux de séparation, mais il est possible qu'il y ait … On ne m'a jamais parlé de ce problème avant, mais c'est possible.» Exprimé en termes plus généraux, pourquoi l'architecture devrait-elle, à son avis, refléter l'existence de différents services ou activités dans une entreprise? «Il y a des espaces de nature très différente, les studios et l'unité de production ont des exigences totalement différentes en matière de lumière, d'espace et d'échelle que les espaces des bureaux, aussi me semble-t-il justifié d'y trouver l'expression de ces différences.»[6]

Canal+ est indubitablement l'un des édifices les plus intéressants et les plus réussis qui aient été construits à Paris ces dernières années. Il présente deux particularités immédiatement décelables qui lui confèrent une certaine impression d'évènement architectural. La première est la «fenêtre urbaine», une grande ouverture à l'extrémité de la façade donnant sur la Seine. Bien que l'architecture de Richard Meier joue souvent sur le rapport vides/pleins, ce cadre curieusement vide intrigue et attire aussi bien ceux qui travaillent dans l'édifice que ceux qui le voient à une certaine distance. Un autre évènement spatial est l'atrium de l'entrée, d'une hauteur de trois étages et entièrement vitré, avec des planchers recouverts d'une nappe de granit brut des Vosges et le bureau de la réception dessiné par Meier lui-même. A peine entrés, ce sont des images de clarté et de qualité architecturale que perçoivent les visiteurs. Elles se retrouvent partout dans l'édifice grâce à divers procédés comme l'utilisation d'un verre extrêmement transparent. Ce genre de matériau, ainsi que le granit, est une indication du budget généreux accordé par le client. Nonobstant ces conditions financières, l'édifice témoigne du grand talent de Meier, que ces éléments structuraux apparents ne suffisent pas à expliquer. L'architecte dut faire face à des contraintes d'aménagement du site lui imposant des hauteurs différentes ainsi qu'à d'autres facteurs limitant sa marge de manœuvre comme les studios et l'espace de production déjà mentionnés, dont il n'a fourni que l'enveloppe extérieure.

Retour en Allemagne

A la fin des années quatre-vingt, Richard Meier, à l'instar de nombreux autres architectes américains, reçut peu de commandes aux Etats-Unis mêmes, excepté bien sûr l'énorme projet du Getty Center. Cela s'expliquait en grande partie par la conjoncture économique. La récession ne toucha pas l'Eu-

city. Completed only between 1884 and 1890, the spire was the last element of a structure first undertaken in 1377. It was designed for 20,000 when Ulm had only 10,000 inhabitants, and to this day, its mass is almost disproportionate to that of the city. Nor were bombs and exaggerated ambitions the only problems of this site. Until the 19th century, a Barefooted Friar's Monastery and church occupied a large part of the square in front of the Ulm Cathedral, but these were demolished in 1874–1875 to allow a clear view of the spire. Over a period of 105 years, the city launched no fewer than 17 design competitions to fill the space left by the Monastery. Until 1987, the site was occupied by a low, undistinguished tourist office and parking area. The 3,500 m² three-story complex built by Richard Meier was dedicated on November 12, 1993, and represents one of his most considerable accomplishments, especially given the difficult circumstances involved (ill. pp. 130–135). Illustrating the complexity of building in any historic area, the Meier project was opposed by the Old Ulm Association, which was against the construction of a modern building on the square, despite the fact that the entire periphery of the area is constituted by poor quality 1950s structures. When asked if this architectural environment was a hindrance, or rather an example of what could be done, Meier replies,

"I think that it's an example for what could be done. I don't think it was a hindrance to the building, to have all those mediocre buildings around it. It certainly would have been nicer to have what was there before it was all bombed and rebuilt, but certainly having the cathedral there was something to respond to. What makes the experience of going through the Exhibition and Assembly Building so unusual and unique, is how you see the cathedral in different ways through the windows and skylights and walkways. In a sense you're constantly aware of the cathedral, even though you're in the Exhibition and Assembly Building. In a sense you see it even better than when you're standing out in the Plaza, because of the way in which the views are framed then disappear and reappear."[7]

Seen from above, in the cathedral spire, the geometric complexity of the building, which is clad in white stucco and Rosa Dante granite from northern Spain, becomes apparent. Segments of three circles interact with a central square to form a flexible interior, given over to an auditorium, tourist office, exhibition spaces and in the adjoining structure, linked by a glassed bridge, a café.

Drawing of the Ulm Münsterplatz, showing the Ulm Stadthaus (1986–1993) in the foreground, and the city's cathedral behind it

Zeichnung des Ulmer Münsterplatzes mit dem Stadthaus Ulm (1986–1993) im Vordergrund und dem Münster im Hintergrund

Etude du Münsterplatz, montrant le centre administratif et culturel d'Ulm (1986–1993) au premier plan, et la cathédrale à l'arrière-plan

Teils 1944 durch Bomben zerstört worden. Nach dem Krieg wurde kein ernsthafter Versuch unternommen, wie etwa in München, die traditionelle Architektur wiederherzustellen. Stattdessen schossen billige Neubauten aus dem Boden, bis zu dem großen Platz vor dem Ulmer Münster, das überraschenderweise den Bomben der Alliierten kaum versehrt entronnen war. Der einzige Turm des Münsters ist mit knapp über 160 m Höhe der größte seiner Art, höher als der Dom von Köln, das sehr viel mehr Einwohner zählt. Der Turm wurde erst zwischen 1884 und 1890 vollendet, als Krönung eines Bauwerks, das 1377 begonnen worden war. Es war für 20 000 Einwohner geplant, als Ulm erst 10 000 besaß, und bis heute wirkt seine Baumasse nahezu unproportional im Verhältnis zur Stadt. Bomben und übertriebene Ambitionen waren freilich nicht die einzigen Probleme dieses Orts. Bis zum 19. Jahrhundert hatten Kloster und Kirche der Barfüßermönche einen großen Teil des Platzes vor dem Münster eingenommen, wurden aber 1874–1875 abgerissen, damit der Blick auf den Turm frei wurde. Über einen Zeitraum von 105 Jahren veranstaltete die Stadt nicht weniger als 17 Entwurfswettbewerbe, um den Platz des Barfüßerklosters zu füllen. Bis 1987 waren hier nur Parkflächen und das niedrige, undefinierbare Gebäude des Verkehrsbüros zu sehen. Meiers dreigeschossiger, 3 500 m² großer Komplex, am 12. November 1993 eingeweiht, zählt zu seinen besten Arbeiten, vor allem angesichts der schwierigen Voraussetzungen (Abb. S. 130–135). Das Gebäude ist ein Beispiel für die Probleme des Bauens in historischem Zusammenhang: Der Entwurf des Architekten wurde vom Heimat-Verein «Alt-Ulm» attackiert, der sich gegen die Errichtung eines Neubaus auf dem Platz wendete, obwohl die gesamte Randbebauung aus minderwertigen Bauten der fünfziger Jahre besteht. Auf die Frage, ob diese Umgebung ein Hindernis war oder eher eine Herausforderung, antwortete Meier: »Ich glaube, es ist ein Beispiel für das, was getan werden konnte. Ich glaube, es war kein Hindernis für das Gebäude, daß alle diese mittelmäßigen Bauten es umgeben. Natürlich wäre es schöner gewesen, das zu haben, was vorher da war, bevor alles zerbombt und wieder aufgebaut wurde, aber natürlich war das Münster etwas, worauf man reagieren konnte. Was den Gang durch das Stadthaus so ungewöhnlich und einzigartig macht, ist die Tatsache, daß man das Münster durch die Fenster und Oberlichter und Gänge so unterschiedlich sieht. In gewisser Weise ist man sich ständig des Münsters bewußt, obwohl man im Stadthaus ist. In gewisser Weise sieht man

rope aussi tôt que les Etats-Unis, et la réputation de Meier en Allemagne, après la construction du musée des Arts décoratifs de Francfort, était faite. En 1986, deux ans à peine après l'achèvement du musée, on lui donna la lourde tâche de construire sur une place que la presse allemande a qualifiée d'«un des sites les plus problématiques du pays», la Münsterplatz à Ulm. Petite ville de 100 000 habitants, lieu de naissance d'Albert Einstein, Ulm perdit 85% de son quartier historique sous les bombardements de 1944. Les conditions étaient si difficiles après la guerre qu'aucun effort véritable n'a été entrepris pour reconstituer le quartier ancien comme cela avait été le cas à Munich, par exemple. A la place, des constructions modernes de mauvaise qualité poussèrent comme des champignons jusqu'à la grande place devant la cathédrale, qui avait échappé comme par miracle aux bombardements. Avec un peu plus de 160 m de haut, la seule flèche de l'église est la plus élevée dans son genre et dépasse celles de Cologne, ville beaucoup plus grande. Construite entre 1884 et 1890, la flèche était le dernier élément d'une structure dont la construction avait commencé en 1377. La cathédrale avait été construite pour 20 000 habitants alors que la ville n'en comptait que la moitié et, aujourd'hui encore, sa masse paraît surdimensionnée par rapport à celle la ville. Ni les bombes ni les ambitions démesurées ne s'avéraient être les seuls problèmes de ce site. Jusqu'au XIXe siècle, une grande partie de la place devant la cathédrale avait été occupée par un monastère de moines aux pieds nus et par une église, mais ils furent démolis en 1874–1875 pour dégager la vue sur la flèche. En 105 ans, la municipalité ne lança pas moins de dix-sept concours de réhabilitation de la place pour combler l'espace vide laissé par le monastère. Jusqu'en 1987, un office de tourisme, construction basse et lourdaude, et une aire de stationnement occupaient le site. Le complexe de trois étages et de 3500 m² construit par Richard Meier fut inauguré le 12 novembre 1993. C'est sans conteste l'une de ses réalisations les plus remarquables, vu les difficultés d'aménagement du site (ill. p. 130–135). Construire dans un quartier historique est une tâche ardue et complexe, l'opposition au projet de Meier en est la preuve: l'Association du vieux Ulm ne voulait pas entendre parler de construction moderne, bien que tout le secteur périphérique fût occupé par des structures de mauvaise qualité datant des années cinquante. A la question de savoir si l'environnement architectural était un obstacle ou un exemple de ce qui pouvait être fait,

Above and below: two interior views of the Exhibition and Assembly Hall, Ulm, Germany, 1986–1993

Oben und unten: zwei Innenansichten des Stadthaus Ulm, Ulm, Deutschland, 1986–1993

Ci-dessus et ci-dessous: deux vues intérieures du centre administratif et culturel d'Ulm, Ulm, Allemagne, 1986–1993

The building is approached through the curving Hirschstrasse, a rather cheap commercial street which leads from the central railroad station. It presents a curved, almost blank facade to pedestrians, who are naturally led into the Münsterplatz, newly redesigned and paved by Meier, along a grid pattern derived from the width of the cathedral tower. As he says, "The completion of the square is the major achievement, making it a real public place after over 100 years. That was something that gave me great satisfaction."

Meier's successful incursion into this particularly complex European environment, with a building whose geometry still conjures up images of De Stijl or other modern art movements, leads to the question of just what might define his work as being American. Richard Meier replies,

"It's hard to generalize, but there are two things. One, I would like to think that there's a certain openness, a certain transparency, a certain lightness that is American. There is also the relationship to the site, the relationship between the building and nature, which may be more American. I don't know that a European would create the kind of siting and the kind of juxtaposition between the park and the building that we created in the case of the Frankfurt Museum of Decorative Arts for example. There is a kind of openness of movement through the building that exists there. I'm also interested in the kind of permanence and specificity which is European."[8]

That said, Richard Meier concedes that the Ulm Exhibition and Assembly Hall is "extremely European. There is no place like that in America," he continues, "nor could we have such a place."

A second building located near Ulm in the almost rural town of Schwendi, was commissioned the year after he won the Münsterplatz competition. The *Weishaupt Forum* (1988–1992, ill. pp. 116–121) is an entrance complex for a manufacturer of gas burners, with a private gallery for contemporary art, a 50-seat lecture hall, a dining area for 260 company workers and a training center. It is indeed very interesting to observe the relations in space developed by this Richard Meier building, between a large sculptural work by Frank Stella hanging in the ground floor area, and industrial burners, neatly aligned on Richard Meier pedestals. Nothing seems out of place. Indeed in the Weishaupt Forum, the extraordinary attention to detail of the architect is brought to the fore. Here, there are never two rows of bathroom tiles which do not match perfectly. Precision is the byword, down to the smallest detail; one is

es sogar besser als draußen auf dem Platz, weil die Ausblicke gerahmt sind und dann verschwinden und wieder auftauchen.«[7]

Vom Münsterturm gesehen, wird die geometrische Komplexität des Gebäudes deutlich, das mit weißem Putz und Rosa Dante-Granit aus Nordspanien verkleidet ist. Drei Kreissegmente sind mit einem zentralen Quadrat kombiniert, so daß flexible Innenräume entstehen. Sie enthalten einen Saal, das Verkehrsbüro, Ausstellungsräume und in dem angrenzenden, durch einen verglasten Gang angebundenen Baukörper ein Café. Man nähert sich dem Komplex über die Hirschstraße, eine nicht sehr niveauvolle Geschäftsstraße, die zum Hauptbahnhof führt. Das Gebäude bietet den Fußgängern eine gekurvte, glatte Fassade und lenkt sie auf natürliche Weise zum Münsterplatz. Der Platz wurde von Meier neu gestaltet und in einem quadratischen Raster gepflastert, der von den Proportionen des Münster-Grundrisses hergeleitet ist. Meier sagt: »Die Vollendung des Platzes ist die Hauptleistung, er ist nun nach über hundert Jahren wieder ein richtiger öffentlicher Platz. Das war etwas, was mich sehr befriedigt hat.«

Daß Meier in dieses besonders komplexe europäische Umfeld mit einem Bauwerk eindrang, dessen Geometrie an De Stijl oder andere Kunstrichtungen der Moderne erinnert, führt zu der Frage, was seine Architektur als amerikanisch definiert. Richard Meier antwortet: »Es ist schwer zu verallgemeinern, aber es gibt da zwei Dinge. Zum einen denke ich, es gibt eine gewisse Offenheit, eine gewisse Transparenz, eine gewisse Leichtigkeit, die amerikanisch ist. Es gibt auch die Beziehung zum Grundstück, die Beziehung zwischen Gebäude und Natur, die vielleicht eher amerikanisch ist. Ich weiß nicht, ob ein Europäer eine solche Anordnung und eine solche Nebeneinanderstellung von Park und Bauwerk realisiert hätte, wie wir es zum Beispiel beim Frankfurter Museum für Kunsthandwerk getan haben. Es gibt eine Art Offenheit der Bewegung im Gebäude, die hier existiert. Ich interessiere mich auch für die Permanenz und Spezifität, die europäisch sind.«[8]

Meier gibt zu, daß das Ulmer Stadthaus »extrem europäisch ist. In Amerika gibt es einen solchen Ort nicht, und wir könnten einen solchen Ort auch nicht haben.«

Für ein zweites Gebäude, nicht weit von Ulm entfernt in der nahezu ländlichen Stadt Schwendi, erhielt Richard Meier ein Jahr, nachdem er den Münsterplatz-Wettbewerb gewonnen hatte, den Bauauftrag. Das *Weishaupt Forum* (1988–1992;

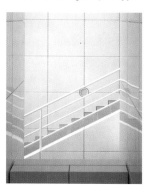

l'architecte répond: «Je pense que c'est un exemple de ce qui pouvait être fait. Je ne crois pas que c'était un obstacle pour l'édifice que d'avoir tout autour ces constructions fort médiocres. Il aurait été certainement plus agréable d'avoir pour cadre ce qui s'y trouvait avant que tout soit bombardé et reconstruit, mais la présence de la cathédrale était une émulation suffisante. Traverser le centre administratif et culturel devient une expérience inhabituelle, unique, grâce aux mille façons d'apercevoir la cathédrale à travers les fenêtres, les lucarnes ou les allées. Dans un sens, on a constamment conscience de la présence de la cathédale, même si on est dans le centre administratif et culturel. On la voit mieux que si on se trouvait sur la place, on en a des vues encadrées qui ne cessent de disparaître et de réapparaître.»[7]

Vu du sommet de la cathédrale, l'édifice habillé de stuc blanc et de granit Rosa Dante du nord de l'Espagne apparaît dans toute sa complexité géométrique. A partir de trois segments de cercles et d'un carré central en interaction, l'architecte a créé un espace intérieur flexible, occupé par un auditorium, un office de tourisme, des espaces d'exposition et, dans une structure contiguë reliée par un pont de verre, un café-restaurant. La séquence d'approche débute par une ligne courbe, la Hirschstrasse, une rue très commerçante qui part de la gare centrale. L'édifice se présente comme une façade courbe, presque nue, aux yeux des piétons qui sont tout naturellement conduits sur la Münsterplatz. Cette place a été rénovée et pavée récemment par Meier, sa grille est basée sur la largeur du clocher de la cathédrale. L'architecte commente ainsi son travail: «L'achèvement de la place est ce qu'il y a de plus important, car elle est redevenue une vraie place après plus de cent ans. J'en ai ressenti une grande satisfaction»[8].

Après le succès de son incursion architecturale dans un environnement européen extrêmement complexe, ainsi qu'en témoigne cet édifice dont la géométrie évoque encore certaines images de De Stijl ou d'autres mouvements artistiques modernes, on est amené à se demander ce qu'il y a de spécifiquement américain dans son art. Il répond lui-même: «Il est difficile de généraliser, mais disons qu'il y a deux aspects. Je pense d'abord à une certaine ouverture, une transparence, une clarté qui sont américaines. Il y a aussi le rapport au site, le rapport de la construction à la nature qui sont peut-être plus américains. Je ne sais si un Européen concevrait la même juxtaposition du parc et de l'édifice que nous avons créée pour le musée des Arts décoratifs de

Interior view of the Weishaupt Forum, showing gas burners on stands designed by Richard Meier, and a wall sculpture by Frank Stella

Innenansicht des Weishaupt Forums mit Gasbrennern auf Objektträgern nach dem Entwurf Richard Meiers und einer Wandskulptur von Frank Stella

Vue intérieure du Weishaupt Forum montrant des brûleurs à gaz exposés sur des piédestaux dus à Richard Meier ainsi qu'une sculpture murale de Frank Stella

tempted to say that here, the grid is the message. Meier rightfully points out, however, the "changing quality of light that illuminates the building's spatial interplay. Architecture, is above all," he continues, "to be experienced with all the senses." Nor does he admit that grids are devoid of higher significance. "Grids," he says, "have existed throughout the history of architecture in different ways. From the Renaissance on we can find the examples of these grids in architecture. They represent a way in which geometrical relationships have been established and held, in defining an ordered meaning to the whole."

The City on the hill
By far the largest project which Richard Meier has ever undertaken, the *Getty Center* in Los Angeles (1985–1997; ill. pp. 156–159) will define his future reputation. A remark which he made about this 88,000 m² six-building complex situated on a 44,5 hectare hilltop site certainly signals that it will stand apart both literally and figuratively in his oeuvre, "In my mind's eye I see a classic structure, elegant and timeless, emerging, serene and ideal, from the rough hillside, a kind of Artistotelian structure within the landscape. Sometimes I think that the landscape overtakes it, and sometimes I see the structure as standing out, dominating the landscape; the two are entwined in a dialogue, a perpetual embrace in which building and site are one. In my mind I keep returning to the Romans – to Hadrian's Villa, to Caprarola, for their sequence of spaces, their thick-walled presence, their sense of order, the way in which building and landscape belong to each other." The reference to Caprarola, the Palazzo Farnese, built by Giacomo da Vignola (1507–1573), near Viterbo in 1559, is particularly unexpected. The very rare pentagonal plan of this castle, laden with occult symbolism, and its rather forbidding exterior, dominating the town, seem quite distant from the grace and light of the Ulm Exhibition and Assembly Hall. In fact, the Getty Center, unlike almost any other Meier structure, will not be white. Due to a Los Angeles law, and a draconian "Conditional Use Permit" which specifically provides that the buildings cannot be white, the architect was obliged to seek another solution for the cladding of the Getty Center. His choice, cleft travertine from Italy, represents a radical departure from any of the smooth surfaces chosen by him in the past. Its surface is rough, and the thick panels are intentionally hung on the facades in an uneven way. Rather than Meier's usual perfection, these strong retaining walls, on a

Abb. S. 116–121) ist ein »Tor«-Komplex für einen Hersteller von Brennern und Heizelementen und enthält eine private Galerie für zeitgenössische Kunst, einen Vortragsraum für 50 Personen, eine Cafeteria für 260 Mitarbeiter und ein Schulungszentrum. Es zeichnet sich aus durch besonders interessante räumliche Beziehungen. Im Erdgeschoß hängt ein großes skulpturales Werk Frank Stellas, und Firmenprodukte wie Industriebrenner sind elegant auf Sockeln Richard Meiers aufgereiht. Nichts scheint am falschen Platz. Tatsächlich hat Meier beim Weishaupt Forum dem Detail eine ganz besondere Beachtung geschenkt. Hier gibt es im Sanitärbereich keine zwei Fliesenreihen, die nicht perfekt zusammenpassen. Präzision ist das Schlüsselwort, bis hin zur kleinsten Einzelheit. Man ist versucht zu sagen, daß hier der Raster die Botschaft ist. Meier weist freilich mit Recht auf die »wechselnde Qualität des Lichts« hin, die »den räumlichen Zusammenhang akzentuiert. Architektur sollte unbedingt«, fährt er fort, »mit allen Sinnen erfahren werden.« Er gibt auch nicht zu, daß dem Raster jede tiefere Bedeutung fehlt. »Raster haben in der gesamten Architekturgeschichte in verschiedenen Formen existiert«, sagt er. »Von der Renaissance an finden wir Beispiele dieser Raster in der Architektur. Sie stellen geometrische Beziehungen her und erhalten sie aufrecht, indem sie dem Ganzen eine geordnete Bedeutung verleihen.«

Die Stadt auf dem Hügel
Das bisher größte Projekt Meiers, das *Getty Center* in Los Angeles (1985–1997; Abb. S. 156–159), wird einen weiteren Beitrag zu seinem internationalen Ruhm leisten. Der 88 000 m² große, aus sechs Bauten bestehende Komplex liegt in einem 44,5 Hektar umfassenden Hügelgelände. Eine Bemerkung Meiers weist darauf hin, daß das Getty Center sowohl im wörtlichen als auch im übertragenen Sinn eine Sonderstellung in seinem Werk einnehmen wird. »Vor meinem geistigen Auge sehe ich einen klassischen Bau, elegant und zeitlos, ruhig und vollkommen aus dem rauhen Hügel hervortretend, eine aristotelische Struktur in der Landschaft. Manchmal denke ich, die Landschaft überwältigt sie, und manchmal sehe ich, wie die Struktur hervortritt und ihrerseits die Landschaft beherrscht. Beide sind in einen Dialog verwickelt, eine ständige Umarmung, in der Bauwerk und Umgebung eins werden. Im Geiste kehre ich immer wieder zu den Römern zurück – zur Hadriansvilla oder nach Caprarola wegen ihrer Raumfolgen, ihrer dickwandigen Präsenz, ihrem Sinn für Ordnung,

Francfort. Il existe une sorte d'ouverture de mouvement à travers l'édifice qui se retrouve là-bas. Je m'intéresse aussi à la permanence et à la spécificité qui sont européennes.» Ceci dit, Richard Meier reconnaît que le centre administratif et culturell d'Ulm est «extrêmement européen. Un lieu de ce genre, il n'y en a pas en Amérique, et il ne pourrait y en avoir».

Un an après avoir gagné le concours du Münsterplatz, l'architecte reçoit la commande d'un second édifice, situé cette fois à Schwendi, petite ville presque rurale des environs d'Ulm. Le *Weishaupt Forum* (1988–1992; ill. p. 116–121) est un édifice d'accès à une usine de brûleurs à gaz. Il se compose d'une galerie d'art contemporain, d'un amphithéâtre de 50 places, d'un restaurant pour les 260 employés de l'entreprise et d'un centre de formation. Il est très intéressant d'étudier les rapports dans l'espace développés par cette construction de Richard Meier entre une grande œuvre sculpturale de Frank Stella exposée au rez-de-chaussée et des brûleurs à gaz qui sont soigneusement alignés sur des socles créés par Richard Meier lui-même. Tout semble parfaitement à sa place. Effectivement, le soin méticuleux accordé au traitement des détails qui caractérise l'architecture de Meier se manifeste ici de façon éclatante. Pas deux rangées de carreaux de salle de bains qui ne s'alignent parfaitement. La précision est le mot d'ordre, jusqu'au moindre détail. On serait presque tenté de dire que la trame est elle-même le message. Mais à juste titre, Meier attire l'attention sur «la qualité changeante de la lumière qui éclaire le jeu spatial de l'édifice. L'architecture, précise-t-il, doit affecter tous les sens». Pour autant il n'admet pas que les grilles soient dénuées d'une importance supérieure. «Les grilles, dit-il, ont toujours existé dans l'architecture, d'une manière ou d'une autre. Dès la Renaissance, on peut en trouver des exemples. Elles ont permis d'établir et de retenir des rapports géométriques en définissant un sens ordonné à l'ensemble.»

La ville sur la colline
Le *Getty Center* (1985–1997; ill. p. 156–159) de Los Angeles, de loin le projet le plus important jamais entrepris par Meier, sera décisif pour la renommée future de l'architecte. Ce centre sera certainement à part dans son œuvre, au sens littéral comme au sens figuré; c'est en tout cas ce que suggèrent quelques observations faites par l'architecte sur ce complexe de 88 000 m² construit sur une colline de 44,5 hectares et comprenant six bâtiments. «Je vois une structure classique, élégante et éternelle,

An aerial view of the model for the Getty Center, Los Angeles, California, 1985–1997, showing the complexity of the plan which can be compared to that of Hadrian's Villa at Tivoli

Luftansicht des Modells für das Getty Center, Los Angeles, California, 1985–1997. Die Komplexität des Lageplans läßt sich mit der Hadriansvilla in Tivoli vergleichen

Vue aérienne de la maquette du Getty Center, Los Angeles, Californie, 1985–1997, soulignant la complexité du plan, comparable à celui de la Villa Hadrien à Tivoli

The Getty Model Shop in Los Angeles where each design change has been incorporated into progressively larger scale models

Die Getty Modellwerkstatt in Los Angeles, wo jede Entwurfsveränderung auf Modelle in immer größerem Maßstab übertragen wurde

L'atelier de maquettes du Getty Center à Los Angeles où chaque modification du dessin fut incorporée dans des maquettes d'études de plus en plus grandes

A view of the cleft travertine facade of the new Getty Center, with the San Diego Freeway below

Ansicht der Fassade des neuen Getty Center aus gespaltenem Travertin, oberhalb des San Diego Freeway

Vue de la façade en travertin du nouveau Getty Center, avec la San Diego Freeway en contrebas

very steep site, call to mind images of Greek or Roman ruins. "That's good," responds Meier. "The Getty will be an institution which is related to Greek and Roman culture certainly. The major portion of Mr Getty's collection was Greek and Roman sculpture, and the design of the existing building is based on a reconstruction of what the Villa dei Papiri in Herculanum might have looked like. So if my architecture has that quality, then perhaps it is all the more appropriate for the Getty."9

Set on a hilltop above the San Diego Freeway, one of the most heavily traveled roads in Los Angeles, the Getty Center looks more like a monastery or a fortress than an open place for learning. Richard Meier emphasizes that the buildings which will soon rise above the travertine walls, with their light-beige metal cladding will give a very different impression, but his architecture has indeed not always clearly signaled its openness. The Getty too, one of the richest cultural organizations in the world, with its museum located on the Pacific Coast Highway in Malibu has not projected an image of greeting the public with outstretched arms. Richard Meier addresses this criticism in a clear way:

"I think the scale, and the way it's sited on the hill, will make people think of an Italian hill town, stone growing up out of the hillside. It has to do with the relationship of the buildings to the terrain. There has been a long debate about the choice of the site since it was selected 10 years ago. Some people think the Getty Center should be in an urban environment, that it should be more accessible, it should be downtown, in some area that needs rebuilding, etc., etc... I think when you go up there, that site is more related to Los Angeles than any other location could be, because of the way you experience the city from the site, and the ways you see the site from different points of the city. The fact that it's visible, the fact that it's prominent, and that you can see it in different ways, is very positive. I think it's extremely well connected to the city and accessible, and I think that those that come there will experience that accessibility. The idea that you have to have an open facade in order to seem open, is not necessarily true. The openness is within."10

The complex layout of the Getty Center is due to the mountainous terrain, and also to the desire of the client to divide its various departments; the Museum, the Getty Center for the History of Art and the Humanities, the Getty Conservation Institute, the Getty Art History Information Program,

wegen der Art, wie Bauwerk und Landschaft sich miteinander verbinden.« Besonders überraschend ist der Bezug zu Caprarola, zum Palazzo Farnese, den Giacomo da Vignola (1507–1573) im Jahre 1559 bei Viterbo errichtete. Der sehr seltene fünfeckige Grundriß des Palazzo, mit okkulter Symbolik befrachtet, und sein nahezu bedrohliches Äußeres, das die Stadt beherrscht, scheinen sehr weit von Anmut und Helligkeit des Ulmer Stadthauses entfernt. Tatsächlich wird das Getty Center, anders als fast alle Bauten Meiers, nicht weiß sein. Aufgrund eines Gesetzes der Stadt Los Angeles und eines drakonischen »beschränkten Nutzungsrechts«, das keine weißen Bauten zuläßt, mußte der Architekt eine andere Lösung für die Verkleidung des Getty Center suchen. Seine Wahl, gespaltener Travertin aus Italien, stellt eine radikale Abwendung von den glatten Flächen dar, die er in der Vergangenheit bevorzugt hatte. Die Oberfläche des Travertins ist rauh, und die dicken Platten sind bewußt ungleichmäßig an den Fassaden angeordnet. So erinnern die starken Stützmauern auf dem sehr steilen Grundstück an Bilder griechischer oder römischer Ruinen. »Das ist gut«, sagt Meier dazu. »Das Getty Center wird eine Institution sein, die sicherlich mit griechischer und römischer Kultur verbunden ist. Der größte Teil von Gettys Sammlung umfaßte griechische und römische Skulpturen, und der Entwurf des bestehenden Gebäudes basiert auf einer Rekonstruktion in der Art, wie die Villa dei Papiri in Herculaneum hätte aussehen können. Wenn also meine Architektur diese Qualität besitzt, ist sie vielleicht umso angemessener für das Getty Center.«9

Das Getty Center liegt auf einem Hügel über dem San Diego Freeway, einer der meistbefahrenen Straßen von Los Angeles. Es wirkt eher wie ein Kloster oder eine Festung als ein offener Ort des Studiums. Richard Meier betont, daß die Bauten, die sich bald über den Travertinmauern erheben, mit ihrer hellbeigen Metallverkleidung einen ganz anderen Eindruck hervorrufen werden. Doch seine Architektur hat ihre Offenheit in der Tat nicht immer deutlich zum Ausdruck gebracht. Auch die Getty Foundation, eine der reichsten Kulturorganisationen der Welt, deren Museum am Pacific Coast Highway in Malibu liegt, erweckt nicht den Anschein, als empfange sie das Publikum mit offenen Armen. Richard Meier entgegnet auf diese Kritik:

»Ich glaube, Maßstab und Lage des Getty Center auf dem Hügel werden die Leute an eine italienische Bergstadt erinnern, mit Mauerwerk, das aus dem Hang wächst. Das hat mit der Beziehung der Bauten zum Terrain zu tun. Es gab eine lange

se dressant, sereine et idéale, sur la colline rocailleuse, sorte de structure aristotélicienne au milieu du paysage. J'imagine que le paysage s'empare d'elle, parfois c'est elle qui se détache du paysage pour le dominer. Ils sont enlacés en un tendre dialogue, en une perpétuelle étreinte jusqu'à ne faire plus qu'un. Je reviens toujours aux Romains, à la villa d'Hadrien, à Caprarola, pour leur séquence d'espaces, leur lourde présence murale, leur sens de l'ordre, leur manière d'unir construction et paysage.» Faire référence à Caprarola, la villa Farnèse construite par Giacomo da Vignola (1507–1573) près de Viterbo en 1559, est très inattendu. Ce château chargé de symbolisme occulte et dominant la ville en contrebas a un plan pentagonal assez rare et des dehors plutôt sévères. Rien à voir avec la grâce lumineuse du centre administratif et culturel d'Ulm. A vrai dire, le Getty Center, à la différence de presque toutes les autres structures de Meier, ne sera pas blanc. En raison d'une loi de Los Angeles et d'un règlement d'urbanisme draconien interdisant expressément l'emploi de la couleur blanche pour les façades, l'architecte a dû chercher une autre solution pour l'habillage extérieur du Getty Center. Il choisit un travertin non poli, ce qui représente une innovation radicale par rapport aux surfaces lisses qu'il affectionne d'habitude. Ce calcaire alvéolé présentant des aspérités, les épais panneaux ont été accrochés exprès de façon inégale sur les façades. Plus encore que la perfection habituelle de Meier, ces murs de soutènement puissants intégrés à ce site escarpé évoquent des ruines grecques ou romaines. «C'est bien», répond Meier. «Le centre Getty sera donc une institution se rattachant à la culture grecque et romaine. Une bonne partie de la collection de M. Getty est constituée de sculptures grecques et romaines, et le plan du bâtiment déjà existant est fondé sur la reconstruction de la villa dei papiri d'Herculanum. Si mon architecture a cette qualité, c'est peut-être ce qu'il fallait pour le centre Getty.»[9]

Se dressant au sommet d'une colline surplombant la San Diego Freeway, une des autoroutes les plus chargées de Los Angeles, le Getty Center ressemble plus à un monastère ou à une forteresse qu'à un lieu ouvert à vocation éducative. Richard Meier souligne le fait que les édifices qui émergeront bientôt au-dessus des murs de travertin avec leur revêtement de métal beige clair donneront une tout autre impression, mais son architecture n'a pas toujours clairement manifesté son ouverture. Le musée Getty, une des plus riches institutions culturelles du monde, situé à Malibu le

Getty Center, model

Getty Center, Modell

Getty Center, maquette

the Getty Center for Education in the Arts, and the Getty Grant Program. "The six buildings of the Center have to serve perhaps a dozen purposes," Meier says. "And yet this complex has to be something more than individual, disparate entities. There must be a sense of the Getty Center. Each building will have its own identity, but each must be a part of the whole." The architect approached this series of problems by creating a plan which resembles that of Hadrian's Villa at Tivoli. Given the frequent references made by Richard Meier to the architecture of the past, and to his own predilection for rotated grids, which often correspond to the axial arrangements of ancient complexes such as the ruins at Tivoli, this connection should not be a real surprise. It does appear here most clearly, however, that Richard Meier is a thoroughly modern architect who feels a deep affinity for the past, be it of this century, or earlier still. When asked why he has related the plan so closely to that of Hadrian's Villa, Meier replies, "I don't think it's a relationship to a monument. I think it's really an expression of permanence. The Getty is an institution of a certain solidity and permanence."

The questions of the permanence of architecture or of art, and of its relation to the work of the past are at the heart of the cultural debate of the late 20th century. Numerous architects and artists have concluded that ours is a time of extreme transience, and that art should reflect the state of the world. Richard Meier, particularly in his recent European work, or in the Getty Center, seems to be looking farther back, and farther forward than most of his colleagues. He has concluded that modernity, even in a geometric mode of expression need not be synonymous with the *tabula rasa* of Gropius. His is an architecture of light and space, in which the visitor or the inhabitant senses an order which is more related to freedom than to any constraint. Beside these elements, the human scale of all of Meier's buildings, even the Hague City Hall or Getty Center is affirmed. Quality and permanence are words which he embraces where others have rejected them.

Where certain forms of Modernism were set aside because of their aridity and lack of concern for inhabitants, Richard Meier has undertaken no less than a rehabilitation of the modern. His jewel-like buildings, and even his "Italian hill town" above the San Diego Freeway speak to concerns which are timeless. Without giving a spiritual dimension to his work that he does not necessarily claim, one can recall the words of the Gospel of Saint Matthew, "A city that is set on a hill cannot be

Debatte über die Wahl des Grundstücks, seit es vor zehn Jahren ausgesucht wurde. Manche denken, das Getty Center sollte in einer städtischen Umgebung liegen, es sollte leichter zugänglich sein, es sollte im Zentrum sein, in irgendeinem Viertel, das Sanierung braucht, usw. usw. Ich glaube, wenn man hinaufkommt, ist der Ort mehr mit Los Angeles verbunden als jeder andere, wegen der Art und Weise, wie man die Stadt von dort erlebt und wie man den Ort von verschiedenen Punkten der Stadt sieht. Die Tatsache, daß er sichtbar ist und daß man ihn auf unterschiedliche Weise sehen kann, ist sehr positiv. Ich glaube, er ist sehr gut mit der Stadt verbunden und sehr leicht zugänglich, und ich glaube, daß alle, die dorthin kommen, diese Zugänglichkeit erfahren werden. Die Vorstellung, daß man eine offene Fassade haben muß, um offen zu erscheinen, trifft nicht unbedingt zu. Die Offenheit liegt im Inneren.«[10]

Das komplexe Layout des Getty Center geht auf das hügelige Gelände zurück, aber auch auf den Wunsch des Bauherrn, die verschiedenen Bereiche zu trennen: Museum, Getty Center for the History of Art and the Humanities, Getty Conservation Institute, Getty Art History Information Program, Getty Center for Education in the Arts und Getty Grant Program. »Die sechs Bauten des Zentrums müssen vielleicht einem Dutzend Zwecken dienen«, sagt Meier. »Und dennoch muß dieser Komplex mehr sein als individuelle, disparate Einheiten. Es muß ein Gefühl des Getty Center da sein. Jedes Gebäude wird seine eigene Identität haben, aber jedes muß Teil des Ganzen sein.« Um dieses Problem zu lösen, entwarf der Architekt einen Grundriß, der dem der Hadriansvilla in Tivoli ähnelt. Angesichts seiner häufigen Rückgriffe auf die Architektur der Vergangenheit und seiner eigenen Vorliebe für rotierende Raster, die oft der axialen Anordnung antiker Komplexe wie der Ruinen in Tivoli entsprechen, ist diese Verbindung keineswegs überraschend. Sie macht vielmehr deutlich, daß Richard Meier, ein durchaus moderner Architekt, eine enge Affinität zur Vergangenheit empfindet, liege sie in diesem Jahrhundert oder noch früher. Auf die Frage, warum sein Grundriß dem der Hadriansvilla so eng verwandt ist, erwidert er: »Ich glaube nicht, daß es eine Verwandtschaft mit einem Monument ist. Ich glaube, es ist in Wirklichkeit ein Ausdruck der Permanenz. Das Getty Center ist eine Institution von einer gewissen Solidität und Permanenz.«

Die Fragen der Permanenz von Architektur und Kunst und ihre Beziehung zur Vergangenheit beherrschen die Kulturdiskussion des späten 20.

long de la Pacific Coast Highway, n'a pas, lui non plus, projeté l'image d'un musée accueillant le public à bras ouverts. Richard Meier répond à cette critique sans ambiguïté: «De par son échelle et sa localisation, les gens penseront à un village italien, à un bloc de pierre émergeant de la colline. Cela s'explique par le rapport des bâtiments au terrain. Le choix du site fait l'objet d'un long débat depuis dix ans qu'il a été choisi. Certains pensent que le Getty Center devrait se trouver dans un environnement urbain, être plus accessible, dans le centre ville ou dans quelque quartier à réhabiliter, etc. Mais quand vous y êtes, vous vous rendez compte que le site est mieux relié à Los Angeles que tout autre endroit. Le fait qu'il est visible, qu'il est proéminent et qu'on peut le voir sous divers angles me paraît très positif. Selon moi, il est très bien relié à la ville et parfaitement accessible. Je pense que ceux qui y viendront sentiront cette accessibilité. L'idée selon laquelle il faut une façade ouverte pour donner une impression d'ouverture n'est pas nécessairement exacte. L'ouverture est à l'intérieur.»[10]

Le plan complexe du Getty Center s'explique par le terrain accidenté, ainsi que par le désir du client de le diviser en plusieurs entités: le musée, le centre d'histoire de l'art et des sciences humaines, le programme d'information sur l'histoire de l'art, l'institut de conservation, le centre d'enseignement et enfin le programme de bourses d'études. «Les six édifices du centre vont servir à une douzaine d'usages» dit Meier. «Et pourtant, le centre Getty est plus que de simples entités individuelles et disparates. Il doit constituer une idée. Chaque édifice aura sa propre identité tout en faisant partie d'un tout.» L'architecte résout cette série de problèmes en créant un plan qui ressemble à celui de la villa d'Hadrien à Tivoli. Ceci n'a rien de surprenant quand on sait que Meier se réfère fréquemment à l'architecture ancienne et qu'il a un goût prononcé pour les grilles décalées les unes par rapport aux autres, ce qui correspond souvent aux arrangements axiaux d'anciens complexes comme celui de Tivoli. Quoi qu'il en soit, il apparaît ici clairement que Richard Meier est un architecte résolument moderne qui se sent une affinité profonde avec le passé, qu'il s'agisse de ce siècle ou de temps plus anciens. Quand on lui demande pourquoi il s'est inspiré du plan de la villa d'Hadrien, il dit: «Je ne crois pas qu'il y ait de rapport avec un monument en particulier. Je pense que c'est réellement une expression de permanence. Le centre Getty est une institution d'une certaine solidité et d'une certaine permanence.»

Richard Meier in front of a model for the Getty Center, taken in his office in Los Angeles, 1994

Richard Meier vor einem Modell für das Getty Center, in seinem Büro in Los Angeles, 1994

Richard Meier photographié devant une maquette du Getty Center dans son bureau de Los Angeles, 1994

hid. Let your light so shine before men..." The permanence in Richard Meier's buildings may be what is most ephemeral, the passing light, the view towards the Pacific Ocean from the Getty Center's Brentwood hill, or from the Ackerberg House. "Between the sea of consciousness and earth's vast materiality lies this ever-changing line of white. White is the light, the medium of understanding and transformative power," says Meier. Art, when it deserves that name, speaks the language of the unspoken. Richard Meier's architecture at its best, is built of light, and Frank Stella's words define his work as well as any others, "Light is life."

Philip Jodidio

Notes/Anmerkungen/Notes

[1] Interview with Richard Meier conducted in the offices of Richard Meier & Partners in Los Angeles on May 16, 1994.
[2] Tom Wolfe, From Bauhaus to Our House, Farrar Straus Giroux, New York, 1981.
[3] Interview with Richard Meier, May 16, 1994.
[4] Ibid.
[5] Ibid.
[6] Ibid.
[7] Ibid.
[8] Ibid.
[9] Ibid.
[10] Ibid.

Jahrhunderts. Viele Architekten und Künstler sind zu dem Schluß gekommen, daß wir in einer Zeit extremer Vergänglichkeit leben und daß die Kunst den Zustand der Welt widerspiegeln sollte. Richard Meier scheint, vor allem bei seinen neueren Bauten in Europa oder beim Getty Center, weiter zurück und weiter nach vorn zu blicken als die meisten seiner Kollegen. Für ihn ist Modernität selbst in einer geometrischen Ausdrucksform nicht unbedingt gleichbedeutend mit der *tabula rasa* von Gropius. Seine Bauten sind Architektur aus Licht und Raum. Der Besucher oder Bewohner empfindet darin eine Ordnung, die der Freiheit näher ist als irgendeinem Zwang. Zudem besitzen alle Werke Meiers, selbst das Den Haager Rathaus oder das Getty Center, einen menschlichen Maßstab. Qualität und Permanenz sind Worte, die ihm viel bedeuten, während andere sie längst verworfen haben.

Manche Formen der Moderne gerieten wegen ihrer Sterilität und ihrer mangelnden Rücksicht auf die Bewohner in Verruf, doch Richard Meier ist so etwas wie eine Rehabilitation der Moderne gelungen. Seine kleinodartigen Häuser und selbst seine »italienische Hügelstadt« über dem San Diego Freeway sprechen Bedürfnisse an, die zeitlos sind. Ohne seinem Werk eine spirituelle Dimension zu geben, die er selbst nicht unbedingt beansprucht, könnte man das Matthäus-Evangelium zitieren: »Eine Stadt, die auf einem Berg liegt, kann nicht verborgen bleiben... So soll euer Licht vor den Menschen leuchten...« Das Konstanteste in Meiers Bauten ist vielleicht das Vergänglichste: das fließende Licht, der Blick auf den Pazifischen Ozean vom Brentwood Hill des Getty Center oder vom Haus Ackerberg. »Zwischen dem Meer des Bewußtseins und der schweren Stofflichkeit der Erde liegt diese ewig wechselnde Linie des Weiß. Weiß ist das Licht, ein Medium der Verständigung und der Wandlungskraft«, sagt Meier. Kunst, wenn sie diesen Namen verdient, spricht die Sprache des Ungesprochenen. Richard Meiers beste Werke sind aus Licht gebaut, und Frank Stellas Worte definieren seine Architektur so gut wie jedes andere: »Licht ist Leben.«

Philip Jodidio

La permanence de l'architecture ou de l'art et leurs relations avec les œuvres du passé sont autant de questions qui se situent au cœur du débat culturel de cette fin de siècle. Nombreux sont les artistes et architectes qui en ont conclu que notre époque était celle de l'extrême éphémère et que l'art devait refléter l'état du monde. Richard Meier, en particulier dans ses réalisations européennes récentes, ou dans le Getty Center, semble regarder plus loin en arrière et plus loin en avant que la plupart de ses confrères. Pour lui, la modernité, même dans une forme d'expression géométrique comme son architecture, ne signifie pas forcément «faisons table rase du passé» comme cela se pratiquait au Bauhaus. Son architecture est celle de la lumière et de l'espace, où le visiteur, ou l'habitant, perçoit une forme d'ordre qui est plus proche de la liberté que de la contrainte. Outre ces éléments, toutes les constructions de Meier, même l'hôtel de ville de La Haye ou le Getty Center, se caractérisent par leur échelle humaine. Qualité et permanence sont ainsi des mots qu'il fait siens alors que d'autres les rejettent.

Tandis que certaines formes du modernisme ont été abandonnées à cause de leur aridité et de leur manque de préoccupations «humanistes», Richard Meier, lui, a entrepris rien de moins que de réhabiliter le moderne. Ses édifices d'une pureté et d'un brillant cristallins, et même sa «ville italienne sur la colline», traitent de thèmes éternels. Sans chercher à donner une dimension spirituelle à son œuvre, qu'il ne revendique pas d'ailleurs, on peut citer l'évangile selon saint Mathieu: «Une ville ne se peut cacher, qui est sise sur la colline. Ainsi Votre Lumière doit-elle briller aux yeux des hommes.» La permanence dans l'architecture de Richard Meier est peut-être ce qu'il y a de plus éphémère, la lumière fugitive, la vue sur l'océan Pacifique du Getty Center perché sur sa colline ou de la maison Ackerberg. «Entre l'océan de la conscience et l'immense matérialité de la terre s'étire la ligne toujours mouvante du blanc. Le blanc, c'est la lumière, le médium de la compréhension et du pouvoir transformateur», dit Meier. L'art digne de ce nom parle le langage de l'inexprimé. L'architecture de Richard Meier à son firmament est toute de lumière, mais laissons le mot de la fin à Frank Stella, qui résume son œuvre mieux que d'autres: «La lumière, c'est la vie.»

Philip Jodidio

Smith House

Darien, Connecticut
1965–1967

Set on a 1,5 acre site overlooking Long Island Sound, the Smith residence is remarkable because of the number of elements of the architect's mature style which it contains. Approached via a bridge, it is closed on one side, and open on the other, which faces the water. Though clad in wood, it is white, with a double-height living room. Undoubtedly influenced by Le Corbusier and other Modernist masters, Richard Meier gives this private house a sense of comfort and space which seems far removed from the functionalist rigor of his European mentors. American architects accepted the unadorned forms of the "International Style" without ever finding much use for the social theories born of periods of extreme turmoil in the Old World.

Das Haus Smith liegt auf einem 1,5 Morgen großen Grundstück mit Ausblick auf den Long Island Sound und enthält bereits viele Merkmale von Meiers reifem Stil. Eine Brücke führt zum Eingang des Hauses. Die eine Seite ist geschlossen, die andere zum Wasser hin offen. Obwohl mit Holz verkleidet, ist das Haus weiß und besitzt einen zwei Geschosse hohen Wohnraum. Meier ist zwar zweifellos von Le Corbusier und anderen modernen Meistern beeinflußt, hat diesem Privathaus aber einen Komfort und eine Räumlichkeit verliehen, die weit von der funktionalistischen Strenge seiner europäischen Mentoren entfernt ist. Die amerikanischen Architekten akzeptierten die schnörkellosen Formen des »Internationalen Stils«, ohne daß sie je viel mit den sozialen Theorien anfangen konnten, die aus den extrem schwierigen Verhältnissen in der Alten Welt entstanden waren.

Construite sur un site de près d'un hectare surplombant le Long Island Sound, la maison Smith est tout à fait intéressante par le fait qu'elle relève de nombreux éléments caractéristiques du style mature de l'architecte. Accessible par un pont, la maison est fermée du côté de l'entrée, et ouverte de l'autre sur la mer. Bien que revêtue de bois, elle est toute blanche, avec un salon à double hauteur. Nettement influencé par Le Corbusier et d'autres maîtres de l'architecture moderniste, Richard Meier donne à cette résidence privée un sens du confort et de l'espace qui paraissent bien loin de la rigueur fonctionnaliste de ses mentors européens. Les architectes américains se sont bien servi des formes dépouillées du «Style international» mais sans jamais avoir adopté les théories sociales nées des bouleversements politiques et sociaux du Vieux Continent.

"Nature is changing all around us, and the architecture should help reflect those changes. I think it should help intensify one's perception of the changing colors of nature, changing colors of the day, rather than attempt to have the architecture change."

»Um uns herum wandelt sich die Natur, und die Architektur sollte helfen, diese Wandlungen zu reflektieren. Ich glaube, sie sollte helfen, die Wahrnehmung der wechselnden Farben der Natur, der wechselnden Farben des Tages zu schärfen und nicht versuchen, sich selbst zu verändern.«

«Tout autour de nous, la nature est en perpétuel changement et l'architecture devrait contribuer à refléter ces changements. Je crois que cela nous permettrait d'intensifier notre perception des couleurs changeantes de la nature, des couleurs changeantes du jour, plutôt que d'essayer de faire changer l'architecture.»

Bronx Developmental Center

New York, New York
1970–1977

Commissioned by the Facilities Development Corporation for the New York State Department of Mental Hygiene, this building shows a closed facade to the relatively hostile, industrial environment. Originally planned as a residential unit for 750 mentally or physically handicapped children, the completed facility is roughly half that size. A reflective natural aluminum finish on the metal panels gives a more mechanical appearance to this building than many of Meier's later structures.

Das Gebäude wurde von der Facilities Development Corporation des New Yorker State Department of Mental Hygiene in Auftrag gegeben. Es wendet der wenig einladenden industriellen Umgebung eine geschlossene Fassade zu. Ursprünglich als Wohnheim für 750 körperlich und geistig behinderte Kinder geplant, ist das fertiggestellte Zentrum etwa halb so groß. Der reflektierende Aluminiumbelag der Metallplatten läßt dieses Gebäude technischer wirken als viele von Meiers späteren Werken.

Cet édifice a été construit pour le Facilities Development Corporation du New York State Department of Mental Hygiene. Ce complexe présente une façade externe fermée sur l'environnement industriel plutôt hostile. Prévu à l'origine pour accueillir 750 enfants handicapés mentaux et physiques, le projet fut réduit finalement de moitié environ. Une peau en aluminium naturel réfléchissant donne à cette construction un aspect nettement plus mécanique que n'ont d'autres réalisations ultérieures de Meier.

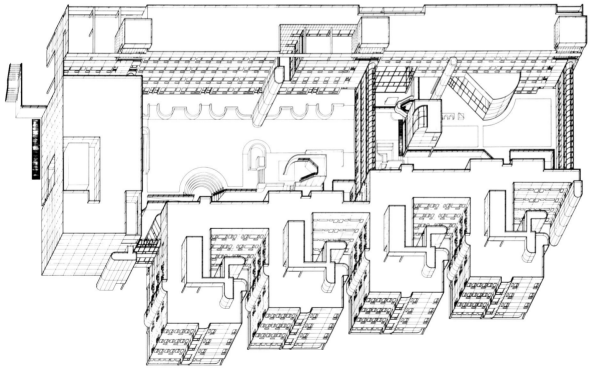

An internal courtyard is more open, as befits both the function and the situation of the structure in a difficult location near the Hutchinson River Parkway. These features are clearly visible on an axonometric view.

Der Innenhof ist offener, passend zur Funktion und zur Lage des Gebäudes auf einem schwierigen Grundstück nahe des Hutchinson River Parkway. Die Situation läßt sich auf der Axonometrie erkennen.

Le centre a une cour intérieure plus ouverte ainsi qu'il convient à la fonction et à la situation d'une structure bâtie sur un site hostile, à quelques pas de la voie express de Hutchinson River. Une vue axionométrique montre clairement ces différents aspects.

Douglas House

Harbor Springs, Michigan
1971–1973

Once again, this house is entered from the rear, this time at roof level, through a bridge. As is the case in the Smith House, it has a high glassed living room which looks out onto the water. It is set in a steep, forested site on Lake Michigan. Perhaps because of the strong contrast between the dramatic natural setting, and the white perfection of the building, this is one of Richard Meier's most frequently photographed buildings. It is also one of the first to go so far in a metaphorical similarity to a ship, with its nautical railings, sweeping decks and projecting smokestacks.

Auch hier führt der Zugang über eine Brücke auf der Rückseite des Hauses, diesmal auf Dachniveau. Wie beim Haus Smith bietet der hohe verglaste Wohnraum einen Ausblick auf das Wasser. Das Haus liegt an einem steilen, bewaldeten Hang über dem Lake Michigan. Wohl wegen des starken Kontrasts zwischen der dramatischen natürlichen Umgebung und der weißen Perfektion des Gebäudes zählt es zu Richard Meiers meistfotografierten Bauten. Es ist zudem eines der ersten, bei dem so viele Schiffsmetaphern wie Relings, auskragende Decks und hohe Schornsteine verwendet sind.

Dans cette maison aussi, l'entrée est située par derrière sous la forme d'un pont tendu au niveau du toit. A l'instar de la maison Smith, elle est organisée autour d'un grand salon vitré à double hauteur, ouvert sur le lac. Elle a été construite sur la rive pentue et boisée du lac Michigan. C'est la construction de Meier la plus photographiée, peut-être en raison du contraste saisissant entre son site spectaculaire et sa blancheur immaculée. C'est aussi la première qui va aussi loin dans la métaphore navale avec ses balustrades façon paquebot, ses larges ponts et ses cheminées saillantes.

Above: the nautical railings and decks of the Douglas House
accentuate the ship-like atmosphere of the design.
Page 58: the LC 1 sling chairs and LC 2 armchairs (Le Corbusier,
Pierre Jeanneret, Charlotte Perriand, 1928) visible in this view of
the fully glazed double-height living room seem appropriate for
the architecture.

Oben: Die maritimen Geländer und Decks des Hauses Douglas
betonen den Schiffscharakter des Entwurfs.
Seite 58: Die Sessel LC 1 und LC 2 (Le Corbusier, Pierre
Jeanneret, Charlotte Perriand, 1928) in diesem vollverglasten,
zwei Geschosse hohen Wohnraum sind der Architektur
angemessen.

Ci-dessus: les ponts et les balustrades façon paquebot
accentuent l'ambiance nautique qui se dégage de la maison
Douglas.
Page 58: les chaises LC 1 à sièges suspendus et les fauteuils
Grand Confort LC 2 (Le Corbusier, Pierre Jeanneret, Charlotte
Perriand, 1928) que l'on aperçoit dans le salon vitré à double
hauteur s'harmonisent très bien avec l'architecture.

The Atheneum

New Harmony, Indiana
1975–1979

An isolated jewel set in the flood plain of the Wabash River, this symbolic building is the starting point for a tour of the historic town founded in 1815 by the Harmony Society. With the arrival of Robert Owen in 1825, it came to be one of the best known utopian communities in the United States. Its interior ramp serving as "chief mediator and armature," this structure bears more than a passing resemblance to Le Corbusier's Villa Savoye (Poissy, France, 1929–1931). There too, an elevated mass is served by ramps with nautical railings. Two grids, with a five-degree shift between them, mark the plan, a frequent characteristic of Richard Meier's buildings, like the recurring ship metaphor. A steel frame building clad with square porcelain-enameled panels, The Atheneum offers a light-filled, heavily articulated space, with numerous views toward the surrounding countryside.

Dieses symbolische Gebäude liegt wie ein isoliertes Kleinod im Überschwemmungsgebiet des Wabash River. Es ist der Ausgangspunkt für eine Tour durch die historische Stadt, die 1815 von der Harmony Society gegründet wurde. Als 1825 Robert Owen eintraf, wurde sie zu einer der bekanntesten utopischen Gemeinschaften der Vereinigten Staaten. Die innere Rampe des Gebäudes, die als »Kern für Kommunikation und Service« dient, erinnert deutlich an Le Corbusiers Villa Savoye (Poissy, Frankreich, 1929–1931). Auch dort werden die Räume durch eine Rampe mit Schiffsreling erschlossen. Zwei um 5° gegeneinander verschobene Raster markieren den Grundriß – ein typisches Merkmal für Richard Meiers Bauten, ebenso wie die häufigen Schiffsmetaphern. Das Atheneum ist aus Stahlrahmen errichtet und mit quadratischen porzellanemaillierten Platten verkleidet. Die Räume sind lichterfüllt und reich gegliedert und bieten viele Ausblicke in die umgebende Landschaft.

Un bel objet isolé, construit à l'abri des crues de la rivière Wabash, c'est ainsi que se présente cet édifice symbolique construit au seuil de la ville historique fondée en 1815 par la Harmony Society. Après l'arrivée de Robert Owen en 1825, elle devait devenir l'une des communautés utopiques les plus célèbres des Etats-Unis. Cette structure a plus d'une ressemblance, grâce à sa rampe intérieure que Meier a qualifiée de «médiateur principal et d'armature», avec la villa Savoye de Le Corbusier (Poissy, France, 1929–1931) qui se présente elle aussi comme une masse élevée sur pilotis servie par des rampes aux balustrades façon paquebot. Le plan de la maison de Meier est conçu à partir de deux grilles, décalées de 5° l'une par rapport à lautre. S'articulant autour d'une ossature en acier recouverte de panneaux émaillés carrés, l'Atheneum est un espace inondé de lumière, lourdement architecturé, multipliant les échappées visuelles sur la campagne environnante.

Hartford Seminary

Hartford, Connecticut
1978–1981

This theological center, which is not devoted to any single denomination, includes a meeting room, chapel, library, classrooms, areas for the faculty, and a bookstore. Square three-foot panels are the basic element of the grid in this building, where transparency and opacity alternate in complex layers. Projecting volumes signal the chapel and library areas. Although Richard Meier has not built many religiously oriented buildings, his white architecture seems particularly appropriate to the study of theology. "Cleanliness" says the old adage, "is next to godliness." The Hartford Seminary building stands out all the more in an area where the neo-Gothic or neo-Colonial styles seem to dominate.

Zu diesem theologischen Zentrum, das keiner speziellen Konfession gewidmet ist, gehören ein Versammlungsraum, eine Kapelle, eine Bibliothek, Seminarräume, Fakultätsbereiche und ein Buchladen. Quadratische, 90 cm große Platten bilden den Grundraster des Gebäudes, bei dem transparente und opake Flächen in komplexen Schichten wechseln. Auskragende Volumen bezeichnen Kapelle und Bibliotheksbereich. Obwohl Meier nicht viele Bauten, die religiösen Zwecken dienen, realisiert hat, scheint seine weiße Architektur dem Studium der Theologie besonders angemessen. »Sauberkeit kommt der Göttlichkeit am nächsten«, wie ein altes Sprichwort sagt. Das Hartford Seminary wirkt umso

eindrucksvoller in einem Gebiet, in dem sonst Bauten im neogotischen oder Neokolonial-Stil vorherrschen.

Ce centre théologique, qui n'est pas voué à une confession en particulier, comprend une salle de réunion, une chapelle, une bibliothèque, des salles de cours, des locaux pour les professeurs et une librairie. Cet édifice, dont la grille a été élaborée à partir de modules carrés de 91,5 cm de côté, joue la carte de la transparence et de l'opacité en couches alternées d'une grande complexité. Des volumes saillants indiquent la chapelle et la bibliothèque. Bien que Richard Meier ait peu construit d'édifices à vocation religieuse, son architecture d'une blancheur immaculée semble propice à l'étude de la théologie. L'édifice du Hartford Seminary se remarque dans cette région où dominent les styles néogothique et néo-colonial du XVIIIe siècle.

Above: the articulation of the facade is not only a formal device but also a reminder that any approach to the spiritual requires the acceptance of a higher order.
Page 67: the simplicity of the chapel and its expression of that which cannot be explained through a flood of light are representative of Richard Meier's capacity to link the architecture of the past to the most modern forms.

Oben: Der Weg zum Eingang führt durch ein vorgestelltes Portal zum Haupteingang. Diese Fassadengliederung hat nicht nur formale Gründe, sondern erinnert auch daran, daß jede Annäherung an das Spirituelle die Akzeptanz einer höheren Ordnung erfordert.
Seite 67: Die Schlichtheit der Kapelle und ihr lichtüberfluteter Ausdruck dessen, was sich nicht erklären läßt, sind charakteristisch für Meiers Fähigkeit, die Architektur der Vergangenheit mit den modernsten Formen in Verbindung zu setzen.

Ci-dessus: l'articulation structurelle de la façade n'est pas qu'un simple arrangement formel mais rappelle aussi que toute approche du religieux implique l'acceptation d'un ordre supérieur.
Page 67: la simplicité de la chapelle et l'expression, sous forme d'un flot de lumière, de ce qui ne peut être expliqué sont très représentatives du talent de Richard Meier à unir architecture du passé et formes les plus modernes.

"I could obviously not create the buildings I do without knowing and loving the work of Corb. Le Corbusier has been a great influence on my mode of creating space."

»Ich könnte meine Bauten zweifellos nicht entwerfen, ohne Corbus Arbeit zu kennen und zu lieben. Le Corbusier hat starken Einfluß auf meine Art, Räume zu bilden, ausgeübt.«

«Je ne pourrais évidemment pas créer mes constructions sans connaître ni aimer le travail de Corbu. Le Corbusier a eu une grande influence sur mon mode de création de l'espace.»

Museum for the Decorative Arts

Frankfurt/Main,
Germany 1979–1985

In many respects, this is one of Richard Meier's most important buildings. Situated on the Museumsufer, on the opposite side of the Main from the downtown area of Frankfurt, and near other cultural institutions, the Museum for the Decorative Arts represents a first for the architect in that the plan integrates an existing 19th century house, the Villa Metzler. As such it represents a break from the Modernist idea of isolated works, and becomes a more urban, public type of building. The 3,5° rotation of the two grids corresponds to the difference between the alignment of the Villa, which itself forms a near perfect 17,6 meter cube, and the embankment of the Main. The dimensions of each quadrant of the project are based on the size of the Villa. Meier's white, elsewhere associated with his Modernist inspiration, here recalls qualities of German Baroque architecture, or even, as he has said, examples of the German porcelain exhibited within. "The project allowed me to make a work of art that forms a meaningful continuity with a broken cultural heritage," says Meier. The heritage he refers to here is undoubtedly that of his own family and others who left Germany in the turmoil leading to World War II.

Dies ist in mancher Hinsicht einer der bedeutendsten Bauten Richard Meiers. Das Gebäude liegt am Museumsufer gegenüber dem Stadtzentrum Frankfurts in der Nachbarschaft anderer kultureller Institutionen und ist für Meier insofern ein Novum, als der Grundriß ein Haus aus dem 19. Jahrhundert, die Villa Metzler, einbezieht. Der Komplex ist betont öffentlich und urban und steht im Gegensatz zur modernistischen Isolation des Bauwerks als eines freistehenden Objekts. Die Verschwenkung der beiden Raster um 3,5° entspricht der Differenz zwischen der Lage der Villa, die ihrerseits einen fast perfekten Kubus von 17,60 m bildet, und dem Verlauf des Mainufers. Der quadratische Raster des Museums basiert in seinen Maßen auf der Größe der Villa. Meiers Weiß, das sonst mit seinen modernistischen Quellen in Verbindung gebracht wird, erinnert hier an die deutsche Barockarchitektur oder sogar, wie er sagte, an die im Inneren ausgestellten Beispiele deutschen Porzellans. »Das Projekt ermöglichte es mir, ein Kunstwerk zu schaffen, das eine sinnvolle Kontinuität zu einem unterbrochenen kulturellen Erbe herstellt«, kommentierte Meier. Das Erbe, auf das er sich bezog, ist zweifellos das seiner Familie und anderer, die Deutschland in der unruhigen Zeit vor dem Zweiten Weltkrieg verließen.

A de nombreux égards, c'est la réalisation la plus importante de Richard Meier. Situé sur le Museumsufer, de l'autre côté du Main par rapport au centre ville moderne, et voisin d'autres institutions culturelles, le musée des Arts décoratifs représente une première pour l'architecte qui intègre dans son plan une maison bourgeoise du XIXe siècle, la villa Metzler. Il représente aussi une rupture avec l'idée moderniste d'œuvres isolées en devenant un type de bâtiment plus urbain et moins privé. Le décalage de 3,5° entre les deux grilles correspond à la différence entre l'alignement de la villa, qui forme elle-même un cube presque parfait de 17,6 m de côté, et le quai du Main. Le format de chaque carré du projet est basé sur les dimensions de la villa. Le blanc, thème de prédilection de Meier, qui dans d'autres constructions paraît d'inspiration moderniste, est à rapprocher ici de l'architecture baroque allemande, ou plutôt, comme il le dit lui-même, des porcelaines allemandes exposées dans le musée. «Le projet m'a permis de créer une œuvre d'art qui exprime la continuité d'un patrimoine culturel brisé», ajoute Meier. Le patrimoine auquel il se réfère est sans nul doute celui de sa famille et de tous ceux qui quittèrent l'Allemagne pendant la période troublée d'avant-guerre.

Pages 68/69: the successively dense layers of Richard Meier's architecture are in this case projected beyond the actual facades of the building, first into a courtyard, but also into the garden stretching out into the Museumsufer site.

Pages 70/71: the straight paths leading into the building accentuate the alignments of the main grids and with their own geometrical precision set the stage for the museum itself.

Seite 68/69: Die zunehmend dichteren Schichten von Meiers Architektur sind hier über die Fassaden des Gebäudes hinaus zunächst auf einen Hof projiziert, aber auch in den Garten entlang des Museumsufers.

Seite 70/71: Die geraden Wege, die ins Gebäude führen, betonen den Verlauf der Hauptraster und bereiten mit ihrer geometrischen Präzision auf das Gebäude selbst vor.

Pages 68/69: les strates de densité graduelle de l'architecture de Richard Meier se projettent, au-delà des façades de la construction, dans une cour et dans le jardin qui s'étend sur le site du Museumsufer.

Pages 70/71: les allées en ligne droite qui mènent au musée accentuent l'alignement des grilles principales et, avec leur précision géométrique, montent les décors pour le musée.

"Modernism doesn't have to throw out the baby with the bathwater. I don't think that everything has to be conceived as being new and different just for difference's sake. I believe that architecture is related to the past, that the present is related to the past, and that we learn from the past in order to move into the future."

»Der Modernismus muß das Kind nicht mit dem Bad ausschütten. Ich glaube nicht, daß alles neu und anders konzipiert werden muß, nur damit es anders ist. Ich denke, die Architektur ist mit der Vergangenheit verbunden, die Gegenwart ist mit der Vergangenheit verbunden, und wir lernen von der Vergangenheit, um uns in die Zukunft zu bewegen.«

«Le modernisme ne doit pas pécher par excès de zèle. Je ne crois pas qu'il faille concevoir à tout prix du nouveau et du différent juste pour la recherche de la différence. Je pense que l'architecture est liée au passé, le présent au futur et que l'enseignement de ce passé nous permet d'aller vers l'avenir.»

"There is a sense of the spiritual in the use of light in all of the great Baroque churches. There, light is central to the experience of the architectural volume; certainly I have used light to a similar end."

»Bei allen großen Barockkirchen liegt eine gewisse Spiritualität in der Verwendung des Lichts. Dort spielt das Licht eine zentrale Rolle für die Erfahrung des architektonischen Volumens. Sicherlich habe ich das Licht zu einem ähnlichen Zweck benutzt.«

«Il y a un sens du spirituel dans le traitement de la lumière dans toutes les grandes églises baroques. La lumière s'y révèle essentielle pour appréhender le volume architectural. J'ai utilisé la lumière dans un but similaire, assurément.»

Above and page 75: the building gives a sense of ordered freedom, rather than one of constrained monotony. To the right, the internal ramp, a device which appears often in Meier's work, as it had earlier in that of Le Corbusier.
Pages 72/73: the Museum for the Decorative Arts represents one of Richard Meier's first direct confrontations with European tradition in the form of the 19th century Villa Metzler which is part of the museum. To the right the glass bridge leading into the Villa from Meier's structure.

Oben und Seite 75: Trotz der scheinbar obsessiven Regelmäßigkeit der Raster erweckt das Gebäude eher ein Gefühl geordneter Freiheit als zwanghafter Monotonie. Rechts die Eingangsrampe, die bei Meier, wie bereits bei Le Corbusier, häufig auftaucht.
Seite 72/73: Inmitten eines Villenviertels aus dem 19. Jahrhundert gelegen, bedeutet das Museum für Kunsthandwerk eine der ersten direkten Auseinandersetzungen Meiers mit der europäischen Tradition. Rechts die verglaste Brücke, die von der Villa Metzler in Meiers Gebäude führt.

Ci-dessus et page 75: il se dégage de cette construction une impression de liberté ordonnée plutôt qu'une monotonie contrainte. A droite, la rampe intérieure, que l'on retrouve souvent dans les réalisations de Meier, comme avant dans celles de Le Corbusier.
Pages 72/73: le musée des Arts décoratifs est l'une des premières occasions pour Richard Meier d'affronter la tradition européenne représentée par la villa Metzler intégrée plus tard au musée. A droite, le pont de verre reliant la villa à la construction de Meier.

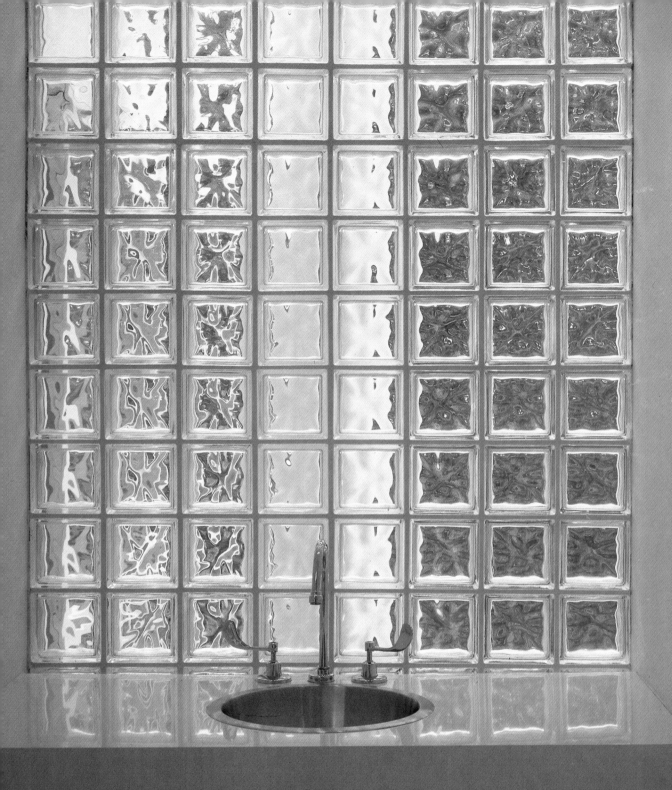

This small house (about 200 m²) has a plan which is based on two unequal squares. As is often the case in Richard Meier's houses, the privacy of the owners is protected by porcelain-enameled metal panels and stucco finishing, whereas reception areas are marked by generous glazing. The sloping site gives the impression from one side that the house is much higher than on the other side. A tubular chimney and walls covered in glass blocks, two other frequent features of Meier buildings, are present in the Giovannitti House.

Der Grundriß dieses kleinen Hauses (ungefähr 200 m²) basiert auf zwei ungleichen Quadraten. Wie so oft bei Meiers Häusern wird die Privatsphäre der Eigentümer durch porzellan-emaillierte Metallplatten und Putzflächen geschützt, während die Empfangsbereiche großzügig verglast sind. Das abfallende Gelände erweckt den Eindruck, daß das Haus auf einer Seite sehr viel höher sei als auf der anderen Seite. Der röhrenförmige Schornstein und die Wände aus Glasbausteinen sind häufig wiederkehrende Elemente in Meiers Bauten.

Cette maison de petite superficie (200 m²) a un plan fondé sur deux carrés inégaux. Comme c'est souvent le cas dans les résidences de Meier, l'espace privé des propriétaires est recouvert de panneaux de métal émaillé et de stuc alors que l'aire de réception se présente comme une grande verrière. Le site en pente donne l'impression que la maison est plus haute d'un côté que de l'autre. Une cheminée tubulaire et des murs en briques de verre, deux thèmes de prédilection de Meier, constituent les caractéristiques principales de cette résidence.

Giovannitti House

Pittsburgh,
Pennsylvania
1979–1983

"I think that it's very difficult, if not impossible, to make forms as beautiful as those which occur in nature. Nature does it better, but we can conceive forms which are inter-related in a way. I think that is really what I am trying to do. I am trying to find a form of construction, which has some meaning in human terms, and relates to the idea of the place."

»Ich glaube, es ist sehr schwierig, wenn nicht unmöglich, so schöne Formen zu entwickeln wie die, die man in der Natur findet. Die Natur macht es besser, aber das, was wir tun können, ist, Formen zu entwerfen, die irgendwie miteinander verbunden sind und die in der Natur vielleicht nicht miteinander verbunden sind. Ich glaube, das ist wirklich das, was ich zu tun versuche. Ich versuche, eine Form des Bauens zu finden, die irgendeine menschliche Bedeutung hat und sich auf die Idee des Ortes bezieht.«

«Il est très difficile à mon avis, pour ne pas dire impossible, de créer des formes aussi parfaites que celles présentes dans la nature. La nature fait ça mieux que nous, mais ce que nous pouvons faire en revanche, c'est concevoir des formes qui, d'une certaine manière, sont inter-dépendantes sans qu'elles le soient peut-être dans la nature. C'est ce que j'essaie de faire, je crois. Je m'efforce de trouver une forme de construction qui ait un sens sur le plan humain et un lien avec l'idée du lieu.»

High Museum of Art

Atlanta, Georgia
1980–1983

Richard Meier has clearly indicated that the central atrium of the High Museum was inspired by Frank Lloyd Wright's Guggenheim Museum. He has taken the occasion though, to criticize the older master by using the atrium for circulation not for the display of art. The High Museum shares the concept of a long entry ramp with The Atheneum, but the structure in Georgia appears to be much more inward looking than the one in Indiana. Though the ramp does represent an invitation to enter, the life of this building is located inside. The High Museum includes about 5,000 m² of exhibition space for works which can be viewed from many different angles, and a 200-seat auditorium. As is so often the case in Richard Meier's architecture, his preoccupation with light, which informs and indeed shapes the space, is amply in evidence here.

Richard Meier hat deutlich darauf hingewiesen, daß das zentrale Atrium des High Museum von Wrights Guggenheim Museum inspiriert ist. Dennoch nutzte er die Gelegenheit zu indirekter Kritik an dem älteren Meister, indem er das Atrium nicht für die Ausstellung von Kunst vorsah, sondern als Versammlungsort für die Bewohner von Atlanta. Wie das Atheneum hat das High Museum eine lange Eingangsrampe, doch der Bau in Georgia ist viel stärker nach innen orientiert als der in Atlanta. Obwohl die Rampe zum Eintritt einlädt, spielt sich das Leben dieses Gebäudes im Inneren ab. Das High Museum verfügt über etwa 5 000 m² Ausstellungsfläche für Kunstwerke, die über den Raum hinweg aus vielen verschiedenen Blickwinkeln betrachtet werden können, und über einen Vortragssaal mit 200 Plätzen. Wie so oft bei Richard Meiers Bauten ist auch hier das Licht als raumbildendes und -belebendes Element eingesetzt.

Richard Meier n'a jamais caché que l'atrium central du High Museum était inspiré du musée Guggenheim construit par Frank Lloyd Wright. Ce fut l'occasion pour lui cependant de critiquer implicitement le vieux maître en évitant d'affecter l'atrium à l'exposition d'art. Cet espace se veut un lieu de rencontre pour les Atlantais. Le High Museum a la même longue rampe d'accès que l'Atheneum, mais l'édifice construit en Géorgie semble plus tourné vers l'intérieur que celui de l'Indiana. Bien que la rampe représente une invitation à entrer, la vie est située à l'intérieur, au cœur du musée. Celui-ci offre environ 5 000 m² d'espaces d'exposition, conçus de telle manière qu'on peut voir les œuvres sous les angles les plus divers à travers tout l'espace intérieur, et un auditorium de 200 places. Comme en témoigne l'architecture de cette construction, la lumière, qui donne une structure et une forme à l'espace, est la préoccupation majeure de Meier.

Page 82 and above: night views of Richard Meier's buildings make their transparency all the more evident. Transparency and openings which invite the viewer's eye to wander from one space to another accentuate a feeling of freedom which is nonetheless structured by the underlying grids.
Pages 80/81: the long entrance ramp, leading diagonally into the building from Peachtree Street, brings visitors toward the central atrium, a convivial space flooded by light, with numerous openings into the museum space itself.

Seite 82 und oben: Nachtansichten von Meiers Bauten machen deren Transparenz besonders deutlich. Diese Transparenz und Öffnungen, die den Blick des Besuchers von einem Bereich in den anderen leiten, schaffen ein Gefühl der Freiheit, das allerdings durch die Basisraster strukturiert wird.
Seite 80/81: Die lange Eingangsrampe, die von der Peachtree Street diagonal zu dem Gebäude führt, bringt die Besucher in das zentrale Atrium, einen geselligen, lichtüberfluteten Ort; von hier öffnen sich viele Wege zum eigentlichen Museumsbereich.

Page 82 et ci-dessus: des vues de nuit mettent en évidence la transparence de l'architecture, et les ouvertures invitant le regard du spectateur à passer d'un espace à un autre renforcent l'impression de liberté que les grilles sous-jacentes ont déjà structurée.
Pages 80/81: la longue rampe d'approche qui va en diagonale de Peachtree Street au musée amène les visiteurs près de l'atrium central, un espace convivial plein de lumière.

"Many times, I have been tempted to use forms which are irregular, but ultimately they always get defined by geometry."

»Viele Male war ich versucht, unregelmäßige Formen zu verwenden, aber letztlich werden sie immer durch die Geometrie definiert.«

«J'ai été maintes fois tenté d'utiliser des formes irrégulières, mais celles – ci relèvent toujours en fin de compte de la géométrie.»

Des Moines Art Center Addition

Des Moines, Iowa
1982–1984

This is an unusual project, in that the addition designed by Richard Meier is directly adjacent to two other distinguished works of modern architecture: Eliel Saarinen's 1948 museum, and I.M. Pei's 1965 addition. Perhaps inspired by the stone of Saarinen's building, Meier here first used granite as a major element of the cladding. There are, naturally, two- and four-foot square metal panels, in particular in the curved areas, but the pink-beige stone finish on this building, intended for permanent and temporary exhibition spaces, adds a new element to Meier's repertoire. "My work," says Meier, "is always related to light, human scale, and the culture of architecture."

Dieses Projekt ist insofern ungewöhnlich, als der von Richard Meier entworfene Erweiterungsbau direkt an zwei andere bedeutende Werke der modernen Architektur grenzt: Eliel Saarinens Museum von 1948 und I.M. Peis Anbau von 1965. Vielleicht durch den Stein von Saarinens Gebäude inspiriert, benutzte Meier hier erstmals Granit als Hauptelement der Fassadenverkleidung. Natürlich gibt es 60 und 120 cm große quadratische Metallplatten, vor allem in den gekurvten Bereichen, doch die rosa-beige Steinverkleidung des Gebäudes, das für Dauer- und Wechselausstellungen bestimmt ist, fügt Meiers Repertoire ein neues Merkmal hinzu. »Mein Werk«, sagt Meier, »ist immer mit Licht, dem menschlichen Maßstab und der Kultur der Architektur verbunden.«

C'est un projet très inhabituel du fait que ce bâtiment annexe dessiné par Richard Meier est adjacent à deux élégants ouvrages d'architecture moderne, le musée construit par Eliel Saarinen en 1948 et le rajout de I.M. Pei en 1965. On ne sait si le matériau employé par Saarinen a inspiré Richard Meier; c'est en tout cas la première fois que celui-ci a utilisé du granit comme composant majeur du revêtement. On trouve bien sûr des panneaux en métal carrés de 60 cm et 120 cm de côté, en particulier sur les surfaces curvilignes, mais la pierre beige rosé de cette construction organisée en espaces d'expositions temporaires et permanentes ajoute un nouvel élément au répertoire de Meier. «Mon travail», dit-il, «est toujours lié à la lumière, l'échelle humaine et la culture architecturale.»

Like a number of Meier's private houses, the Des Moines Art Center reveals greater volume and height on one side than on the other. This view shows the almost musical complexity of the forms.

Wie manche Privathäuser Richard Meiers besitzt das Des Moines Art Center auf einer Seite mehr Höhe und Volumen als auf der anderen. Diese Ansicht macht die nahezu musikalische Komplexität der Formen deutlich.

A l'instar d'un certain nombre de résidences privées construites par Meier, le volume et la hauteur du Des Moines Art Center sont plus importants d'un côté que de l'autre. Cette image montre bien la complexité presque musicale de ses formes.

Above and page 87: the basic paneling units of the Art Center Addition are four-foot squares, with white, porcelain-enameled steel covering the curved volumes in particular, and gray granite for the central cube of the main part of the addition.

Oben und Seite 87: Die Fassadenverkleidung des Erweiterungsbaus besteht aus 120 cm großen quadratischen Elementen. Bei den gekurvten Volumen ist weißer, porzellan-emaillierter Stahl verwendet, bei dem zentralen Kubus des Erweiterungsbaus dagegen grauer Granit.

Ci-dessus et page 87: le module de base du panneautage mesure 1,20 m. Le revêtement est constitué d'acier émaillé blanc, en particulier sur les volumes arrondis, et de granit gris sur la partie centrale de forme cubique.

"I think that the fallacy that Frank Lloyd Wright perpetrated for many years had to do with the nature of materials. He claimed to use what are called natural materials, but the minute you cut down that tree and you use it in construction, it is no longer alive, it is no longer growing, it is inert. The materials we're using in construction are not natural, they are not changing with the seasons, or with the time of day. What we make is static in its material quality. Therefore, it's a counterpoint to nature."

»Ich glaube, der Irrtum, dem Frank Lloyd Wright jahrelang verfallen war, hatte mit der Natur der Materialien zu tun. Er behauptete, er benutze sogenannte natürliche Materialien, aber in der Minute, in der man diesen Baum fällt und beim Bau verwendet, lebt er nicht mehr, wächst er nicht mehr, ist er tot. Die Materialien, die wir beim Bauen verwenden, sind nicht natürlich, sie wechseln nicht mit den Jahres- oder Tageszeiten. Was wir machen, ist in seiner materiellen Qualität statisch. Deshalb ist es ein Kontrapunkt zur Natur.«

«L'erreur commise par Frank Lloyd Wright, il y longtemps déjà, portait sur la nature des matériaux. Il prétendait utiliser des matériaux dits naturels, mais dès l'instant où vous coupez un arbre et l'utilisez pour construire, il a cessé de vivre, il ne pousse plus, il est inerte. Les matériaux que nous utilisons dans la construction ne sont pas naturels, ils ne changent pas au rythme des saisons ni des journées. Ce que nous créons est statique dans sa substance matérelle. Il est donc un contrepoint à la nature.»

Malibu's Pacific Coast Highway, where this house is located, is a narrow strip of land between the mountains and the sea. Along it, a remarkable hodge-podge of architectural styles jostle for attention. Fairly private and closed on the Highway side, the Ackerberg House opens out, after a series of internal courtyards, onto a spectacular view of the ocean front. The guest wing and the Highway facade underwent modifications, carried out by Richard Meier in the spring of 1994. This seems to be an ideal location for the substantial collection of contemporary art which the Ackerbergs display in the house. Nor does Richard Meier's orchestration of white geometrical forms interfere with the display of works which may be very figurative, such as the nudes of Robert Graham.

Der Pacific Coast Highway in Malibu, an dem dieses Haus liegt, ist ein schmaler Landstreifen zwischen den Bergen und dem Meer. Entlang der Straße machen sich Häuser in kunterbuntem Stilgemisch die Aufmerksamkeit streitig. Das Haus Ackerberg ist an der Straßenseite relativ geschlossen, öffnet sich aber nach einer Reihe innerer Höfe zu einem spektakulären Ausblick auf den Ozean. Das Gästehaus und die Straßenfassade wurden im Frühjahr 1994 von Richard Meier umgebaut. Das Haus Ackerberg ist ein idealer Ort für die bemerkenswerte Sammlung moderner Kunst, die die Eigentümer hier ausstellen. Meiers weiße geometrische Formen geraten auch mit sehr figurativen Werken wie den Akten Robert Grahams nicht in Konflikt.

Cette maison est située à Malibu sur la Pacific Coast Highway, une route formant une étroite bande de terre entre les collines et la mer. Tout le long de la route, ce n'est qu'un bric-à-brac de styles architecturaux rivalisant pour attirer l'attention. Fermée et privée du côté de la route, la maison s'ouvre sur une vue spectaculaire du front de mer après une séquence de cours intérieures. L'aile réservée aux amis et la façade côté route ont subi des modifications que Richard Meier a menées à bonne fin au printemps 1994. C'est un endroit qui paraît idéal pour l'importante collection d'art contemporain que les Ackerberg ont exposée dans la maison, et ce d'autant plus que l'orchestration des formes géométriques blanches n'interfère pas le moins du monde avec les œuvres exposées.

Ackerberg House

Malibu, California
1984–1986

"White is the ephemeral emblem of perpetual movement. The white is always present but never the same, bright and rolling in the day, silver and effervescent under the full moon of New Year's Eve. Between the sea of consciousness and earth's vast materiality lies this ever-changing line of white. White is the light, the medium of understanding and transformative power."

»*Weiß ist das vergängliche Symbol ständiger Bewegung. Weiß ist immer gegenwärtig, aber nie gleich, hell und unstet am Tage, silbrig und schäumend unter dem Vollmond der Sylvesternacht. Zwischen dem Meer des Bewußtseins und der schweren Stofflichkeit der Erde liegt diese ewig wechselnde Linie des Weiß. Weiß ist das Licht, ein Medium der Verständigung und der Wandlungskraft.*«

«*Le blanc est l'emblème éphémère du mouvement perpétuel. Le blanc est toujours présent mais n'est jamais le même, brillant et ondoyant dans la clarté du jour, argent et effervescent sous les rayons de la pleine lune au nouvel an. Entre l'océan de la conscience et l'immense matérialité de la terre s'étire la ligne toujours mouvante du blanc. Le blanc, c'est la lumière, le médium de la compréhension et du pouvoir transformateur.*»

Pages 90/91: the white precision of Richard Meier's architecture takes on the character of the light.
Pages 92/93: the double-height living room of the Ackerberg House is designed to fully take advantage of the extraordinary view toward the Pacific Ocean.

Seite 90/91: Die weiße Präzision von Meiers Architektur fängt nicht nur die Lichtqualität eines jeden Augenblicks ein, sondern bildet auch einen sehr guten Hintergrund für Kunstwerke wie hier Robert Grahams Aktskulptur.
Seite 92/93: Der zwei Geschosse hohe Wohnraum des Hauses Ackerberg ist so orientiert, daß er einen großartigen Ausblick auf den Strand und die Weite des Pazifischen Ozeans bietet.

Pages 90/91: la blanche précision de l'architecture de Richard Meier prend le caractère changeant de la lumière.
Pages 92/93: le salon à double hauteur est conçu de manière à tirer parti au maximum du panorama extraordinaire qu'on a du site sur la plage et de l'immense espace libre que représente le Pacifique.

Westchester House

Westchester County,
New York
1984–1986

As in the Grotta House, the client who built this house, located on a spectacular 40-hectare site, is an old friend of Richard Meier, which undoubtedly facilitated the design process. Once again, the Westchester House is related in its plan to the Smith House, a fact which accentuates the almost repetitive nature of Meier's design process. The architect separates the "public" spaces, here delineated by curved volumes, from the "private" rectilinear forms. The curved areas give a needed relief as opposed to the stricter lines of the rectangular ones. A design detail of some interest is the use of a small amount of stained glass in the upper level of the living room, like a distant echo of Frank Lloyd Wright's windows.

Wie Grotta ist der Bauherr dieses Hauses, das auf einem spektakulären, 40 Hektar großen Grundstück liegt, ein Jugendfreund Richard Meiers, was den Entwurfsprozeß zweifellos erleichterte. Auch das Haus Westchester ist im Grundriß dem Haus Smith verwandt – eine Tatsache, die auf den nahezu repetitiven Charakter von Meiers Entwürfen hinweist. Zudem trennt der Architekt wiederum die »öffentlichen« Bereiche, hier durch gekurvte Volumen gekennzeichnet, von den »privaten«. Die gekurvten Umrisse sorgen für den notwendigen Ausgleich zu den strengeren rechteckigen Formen. Ein interessantes Detail ist eine kleine Partie mit farbigem Glas im oberen Bereich des Wohnraums, die wie ein fernes Echo der Fenster Frank Lloyd Wrights wirkt.

Le propriétaire de cette résidence, construite sur un site splendide d'une superficie de 40 hectares, est, comme Louis Grotta, un vieil ami de Richard Meier, ce qui a dû faciliter la conception du projet, on s'en doute. La maison Westchester est apparentée elle aussi à la maison Smith par son plan, fait qui souligne le caractère répétitif du processus de conception chez Richard Meier. Dans cette maison aussi, l'architecte sépare les espaces publics, représentés par des volumes courbes, des espaces privés, autre thème récurrent de son architecture. Les surfaces courbes donnent une note plus légère à l'ensemble en opposition aux lignes sévères des surfaces rectangulaires. Il se trouve parmi les «effets de structure» un détail assez intéressant: une citation de vitrail dans la partie supérieure de la verrière du salon, comme une lointaine réminiscence des fenêtres de Frank Lloyd Wright.

Pages 94/95: in its appearance, this house, one of the last of Meier's private residences in the 1980s seems more massive than some of his other work, perhaps in part because of the heavy masonry walls, meant to echo fieldstone walls which exist on the site.

Seite 94/95: Dieses Haus, eines der letzten privaten Wohnhäuser Meiers aus den achtziger Jahren, wirkt massiver als manche seiner anderen Arbeiten, vielleicht wegen der schweren Wände aus Mauerwerk, die sich auf die vorhandenen Feldsteinmauern des Grundstücks beziehen.

Pages 94/95: cette maison compte parmi les dernières résidences privées construites par Meier dans les années 80. Elle a une allure plus massive que bien d'autres, peut-être en partie à cause des murs en maçonnerie lourde qui ont été conçus pour répondre en écho aux murailles de pierre se trouvant sur le site.

Pages 96/97: as in other Meier houses, the spaces intended for reception of guests are more open than the actual residence areas. A dining room with relatively little furniture is orientated toward the remarkable landscape of the site. Though it seems antithetical to the setting in its geometric strength, the house thus reveals its function as an homage to that setting.

Seite 96/97: Wie bei anderen Häusern Meiers sind die Räume für den Empfang von Gästen offener als die eigentlichen Wohnbereiche. Ein Speisezimmer mit relativ wenigen Möbeln öffnet sich weit auf die bemerkenswerte Landschaft. So stellt das Haus trotz seiner kontrastierenden geometrischen Strenge eine Hommage an seine Umgebung dar.

Pages 96/97: ici comme dans toute maison de Meier, l'espace réservé aux invités est plus ouvert que l'aire de résidence des propriétaires. Une salle à manger peu meublée a vue sur le paysage extraordinaire du site. Bien qu'elle paraisse à l'opposé du site par sa puissante géométrie, cette maison constitue ainsi un hommage rendu au cadre naturel.

Bridgeport Center

Bridgeport, Connecticut
1984–1989

An idea which has fascinated a number of architects in recent years is that of creating a sort of "city in miniature" in a single group of buildings. Richard Meier's design for Bridgeport was intended to renew an urban stretch along Interstate 95, the main highway leading from New York to Boston. The complex contains a sixteen-story office tower, his highest building to date, although a higher structure is now being studied for the Compaq computer company in Texas. A five-story atrium provides a point of "internal focus." By the standards of Richard Meier, the Bridgeport Center is unusually colorful, clad in white and gray porcelain steel panels, red granite and glass.

Eine Idee, die in den letzten Jahren viele Architekten fasziniert hat, ist die Schaffung einer Art »Miniaturstadt« in einer einzigen Gebäudegruppe. Richard Meiers Entwurf für Bridgeport war zur Sanierung eines Stadtgebiets entlang der Interstate 95 gedacht, der Hauptautobahn von New York nach Boston. Zu dem Komplex gehört ein sechzehn Geschosse hoher Büroturm, Meiers bis dahin höchstes Gebäude. Ein fünf Geschosse hohes Atrium sorgt für einen »inneren Mittelpunkt«. An Meiers Maßstäben gemessen, wirkt das Bridgeport Center ungewöhnlich farbenfreudig. Es ist mit weißen und grauen emaillierten Metallplatten, rotem Granit und Glas verkleidet.

C'est une idée qui a fasciné de nombreux architectes ces dernières années: faire une «cité en miniature» d'un complexe composé de bâtiments hétérogènes. L'étude de Bridgeport était destinée à rénover une zone urbaine s'étirant le long de l'Interstate 95, l'autoroute reliant New York à Boston. Le complexe se présente comme une tour de bureaux de seize étages, la plus haute construction de Meier jusqu'à ce jour . Un atrium d'une hauteur de cinq étages est le point de «convergence interne». Par rapport aux qualités habituelles des constructions de Meier, le Bridgeport Center est étonnamment coloré, recouvert de panneaux en acier blancs et gris, de granit rouge et de verre.

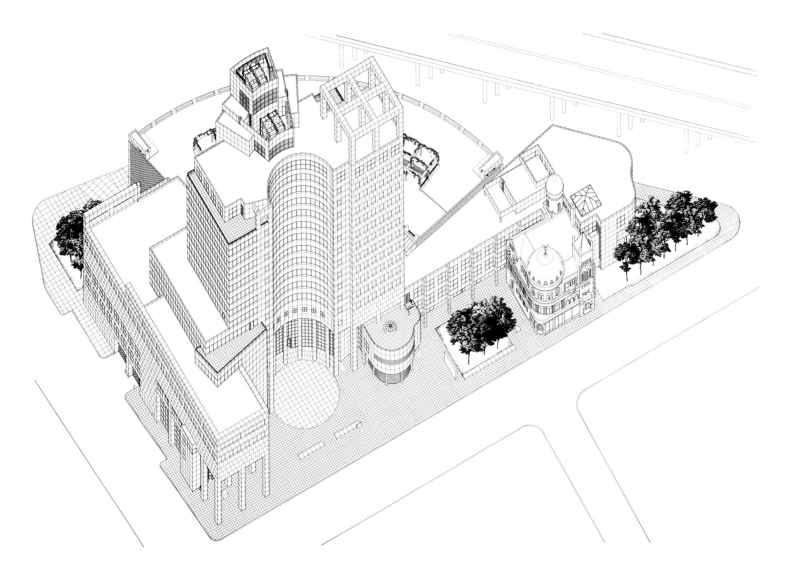

"I think grids have existed throughout the history of architecture in different ways. From the Renaissance on we can find the examples of these grids in architecture. They represent a way in which geometrical relationships have been established and held, in defining an ordered meaning to the whole."

»Raster haben in der gesamten Architekturgeschichte in verschiedenen Formen existiert. Seit der Renaissance finden wir Beispiele dieser Raster in der Architektur. Sie stellen geometrische Beziehungen her und erhalten sie aufrecht, indem sie dem Ganzen eine geordnete Bedeutung verleihen.«

«Les grilles ont toujours existé dans l'architecture, d'une manière ou d'une autre. A partir de la Renaissance, on peut en trouver des exemples dans les ouvrages d'architecture. Elles ont permis d'établir et de retenir des rapports géométriques en définissant un sens ordonné à l'ensemble.»

Mr. Grotta, a childhood friend of Meier's shares a vision with his wife of their house which allows for no stray objects, only the architecture, necessary furniture, and their own crafts collection. They are also almost fanatical admirers of Richard Meier's architecture, although they also interviewed other architects before settling on their friend. Set on a beautiful 2,5 hectare sloping meadow land site in a particularly rural area of New Jersey, the main internal space of the house is structured around a central cylindrical 6,7 meter high living room. Like a reminder of earlier Meier houses, a bridge enters the house from the rear, where the original design called for a swimming pool. A covered walkway connects the house to a parking area, and serves as the main entrance. Aside from the gray paneling, another unusual surface feature of the Grotta House is the use of ground-faced concrete block at the back and kitchen side of the house.

Grotta, ein Jugendfreund des Architekten, und seine Frau haben eine Vision von ihrem Haus, die keine umherliegenden Gegenstände zuläßt – nur die Architektur, die notwendigen Möbel und ihre eigene Sammlung von Kunsthandwerk. Sie sind nahezu fanatische Bewunderer Meiers, obwohl die Grottas auch andere Architekten konsultierten, bevor sie sich für ihren Freund entschieden. Das Haus liegt auf einem schönen, 2,5 Hektar großen abfallenden Wiesengelände in einem besonders ländlichen Gebiet New Jerseys. Das Innere des Hauses ist um einen zentralen zylindrischen, 6,70 m hohen Wohnraum angeordnet. Wie bei früheren Häusern Meiers liegt eine Eingangsbrücke an der Rückseite des Hauses, wo ursprünglich ein Schwimmbecken vorgesehen war. Ein überdeckter Gang verbindet das Haus mit einem Parkplatz und dient als Haupteingang. Abgesehen von den grauen Platten ist beim Haus Grotta die Verwendung von Betonstein an der Rückseite und Küche des Hauses ungewöhnlich.

M. Grotta, un ami d'enfance de l'architecte, et sa femme avaient une vision précise de leur maison: débarrassée d'objets parasites, vivant de sa seule architecture, meublée juste du nécessaire et de leur collection d'objets d'art populaire. La maison est construite en pleine campagne du New Jersey, sur un très beau site de 2,5 hectares de prairie en pente douce. Elle est structurée autour du salon, un espace cylindrique central de 6,7 m de haut. Sorte de réminiscence des premières réalisations de Meier, l'accès à la maison peut se faire par un pont placé à l'arrière, à l'endroit exact où il était prévu de construire une piscine. Un passage couvert relie la maison au parking et sert d'entrée principale. Pour la structure extérieure, l'architecte a utilisé deux matériaux inhabituels: des panneaux émaillés de couleur grise sur la façade de devant et des parpaings de béton brut derrière la maison et du côté de la cuisine.

Grotta House

Harding Township,
New Jersey
1985–1989

Madison Square Garden Site Redevelopment

New York, New York
1987

This unbuilt project was designed for a competition for redevelopment of the present Madison Square Garden site in Manhattan into office buildings. Richard Meier proposed the construction of three related towers, with the one on the south reaching some 72 stories. The 38-story east tower and the rest of the complex would have been elevated on a podium. Unlike anything Richard Meier has in fact built, this complex demonstrates both the flexibility of his style, and his ability to design large, urban projects.

Dieses nicht realisierte Projekt entstand für einen Wettbewerb zur Umgestaltung des jetzigen Madison Square Garden (Manhattan) in Bürogebäude. Richard Meier schlug drei miteinander verbundene Türme vor, deren südlicher 72 Geschosse haben sollte. Der 38-geschossige Ostturm und der Rest des Komplexes sollten auf einen erhöhten Sockel plaziert werden. Diese Gebäudegruppe, die anders ist als alles, was Meier je gebaut hat, demonstriert seine Flexibilität im Entwurf und seine Fähigkeit, große urbane Projekte zu planen.

Ce projet jamais réalisé avait été conçu par Richard Meier à l'occasion d'un concours pour le réaménagement de Madison Square Garden à Manhattan en immeubles de bureaux. L'étude prévoyait la construction de trois tours reliées entre elles, dont l'une au sud du site aurait atteint 72 étages. La tour de 38 étages construite à l'est et le reste du complexe auraient été posés sur un socle. Fort différent de ce que Richard Meier a réalisé jusque-là, ce complexe témoigne de la flexibilité de son style et de sa capacité à concevoir des projets urbains à grande échelle.

Royal Dutch Paper Mills Headquarters

Hilversum, The Netherlands
1987–1992

This relatively small office and reception complex is located in one of the best known residential areas in Holland. Midway between Amsterdam and The Hague, it is near Schiphol Airport, and is visible from the A27 highway. The headquarters building, originally intended for the directors of the KNP-BT paper company, consists of two structures – a four-story cubic reception building and an 80 m long two-story office block which is elevated on pilotis. A light beige Spanish limestone wall marks the separation between the two elements. Called "un-Dutch" by a national newspaper, the KNP-BT building is in fact not far from the Schröder House, built by Gerrit Rietveld in Utrecht in 1924, in collaboration with his client, Truus Schröder. Rietveld's first building bears some resemblance to Meier's works, as does the apartment building on Erasmuslaan in Utrecht, also built by Rietveld in collaboration with Truus Schröder (1930–1935). KNP-BT chose Meier in 1987 to build this complex without a competition, one year after he was designated for the

Dieser relativ kleine Büro- und Empfangskomplex liegt nahe dem Flughafen Schiphol in einem der bekanntesten Wohngebiete Hollands zwischen Amsterdam und Den Haag und ist von der Autobahn A27 zu sehen. Die Hauptverwaltung, ursprünglich für die Direktoren der Papierfabrik KNP-BT bestimmt, besteht aus zwei Bauten – einem kubischen viergeschossigen Empfangsgebäude und einem 80 m langen zweigeschossigen Büroflügel, der sich auf Pilotis erhebt. Eine hellbeige Wand aus spanischem Kalkstein markiert die Trennung zwischen den beiden Gebäudeteilen. KNP-BT, von einer Lokalzeitung als »unholländisch« bezeichnet, ist nicht weit von Haus Schröder entfernt, das Gerrit Rietveld 1924 zusammen mit der Bauherrin Truus Schröder in Utrecht errichtete. Rietvelds erster Bau hat einige Verwandtschaft mit Meiers Arbeiten, ebenso wie das Mietshaus am Erasmuslaan in Utrecht, das Rietveld ebenfalls in Zusammenarbeit mit Truus Schröder baute (1930–1935). KNP-BT wählte Meier 1987 ohne Ausschreibung eines Wettbewerb als

Ce complexe de bureaux d'une échelle plutôt modeste est situé dans une des zones résidentielles les plus connues de Hollande. Construit non loin de l'aéroport de Schiphol, entre Amsterdam et La Haye, on l'aperçoit de l'autoroute voisine A27. Le siège, prévu au départ pour les administrateurs de KNP-BT, se compose de deux entités, un bâtiment de forme cubique de 4 étages et une barre de 2 étages et 80 m de long posée sur pilotis. Un mur en calcaire d'Espagne beige clair sert de séparation entre les deux structures. Bien que qualifié de «non-hollandais» par un journal local, l'immeuble de KNP-BT a en fait une certaine affinité avec la maison Schröder que Gerrit Rietveld construisit en 1924 en collaboration avec le propriétaire, Truus Schröder. Les constructions de Meier ont des points communs avec cette première réalisation de l'architecte hollandais ainsi qu'avec son bâtiment sur Erasmuslaan à Utrecht, fruit aussi d'une coopération avec Schröder. Meier fut choisi en 1987 par le KNP-BT sans concours préalable, un an

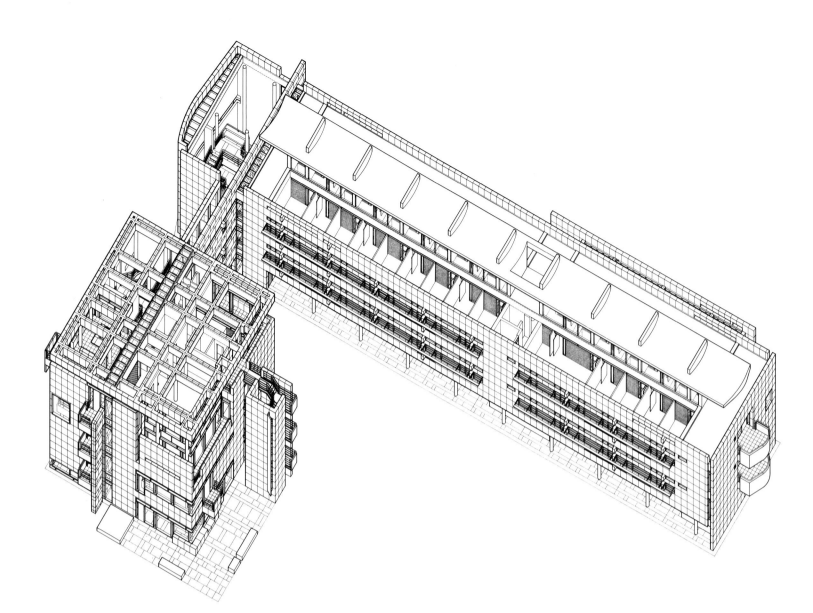

Hague City Hall project. The design work was carried out between April 1989 and December 1990, construction between December 1990 and March 1992. "Architecture is the subject of my architecture," says Richard Meier, and perhaps because of the ample means provided by the client, this building is full of architecture. The complex articulation of the facades and the unexpected ways in which angles meet within the building, are elements which might lead the visitor to feel that a somewhat simpler approach might have been warranted.

Architekten, ein Jahr, nachdem er den Wettbewerb für das Den Haager Rathaus gewonnen hatte. Die Planung fand zwischen April 1989 und Dezember 1990 statt, der Bau zwischen Dezember 1990 und März 1992. »Architektur ist das Thema meiner Architektur«, sagt Richard Meier, und vielleicht wegen der üppigen Mittel, die der Bauherr zur Verfügung stellte, ist dieses Gebäude voll von Architektur. Die komplexe Artikulation der Fassaden und die überraschenden Überschneidungen von Flächen im Inneren könnten beim Besucher sogar den Eindruck erwecken, daß auch eine etwas einfachere Lösung zu vertreten gewesen wäre.

après avoir été désigné pour bâtir l'hôtel de ville de La Haye. Les études du projet définitif furent menées entre avril 1989 et décembre 1990, la construction entre décembre 1990 et mars 1992. «L'architecture est le sujet de mon architecture», dit Richard Meier, et en raison peut-être des moyens importants mis à la disposition de l'architecte par le client, cette construction est chargée d'architecture. L'articulation complexe des façades et la manière inattendue dont les angles se rejoignent à l'intérieur de la structure sont des éléments qui donnent au visiteur l'impression qu'une approche un peu plus simple se serait justifiée.

"You can't ignore things that you have seen in the past, that have impressed you, or extraordinary works of architecture. To say that there is direct reference would be wrong, but I wanted to have some tautness of Dutch architecture. It's a reference to many architects, but it's not intended as a direct reference to anyone."

»Man kann Dinge nicht ignorieren, die man in der Vergangenheit gesehen hat, die einen beeindruckt haben, oder außergewöhnliche Werke der Architektur. Es wäre falsch zu sagen, daß es einen direkten Bezug gibt, aber ich wollte etwas von der Straffheit der holländischen Architektur haben. Es hat Bezüge zu vielen Architekten, aber es ist nicht als direkter Bezug auf irgend jemanden gedacht.«

«Vous ne pouvez ignorer les choses que vous avez vues dans le passé, qui vous ont impressionné ou les ouvrages d'architecture remarquables. Il serait faux de parler de référence directe, mais je souhaitais avoir un peu de la tension qui caractérise l'architecture hollandaise. C'est une référence à de nombreux architectes, mais elle ne se veut pas une référence directe à l'un d'entre eux.»

City Hall and Central Library

The Hague, The Netherlands
1986–1995

Clad inside and out with white 85 x 180 cm porcelain-enameled metal panels, this very large group of buildings is located near Centraal Station in The Hague, and the Ministries of Justice and Foreign Affairs on a difficult wedge-shaped site. The alignment of the city streets and the site inspired Richard Meier to introduce a 12,5° rotation in the two main grids of the structure, corresponding to a 12-story office "slab" and a 10-story block. Between these elements, he has placed the most spectacular feature of the building, a 47 meter high glassed atrium, which will be the largest space of its kind in Europe. The City Hall and Central Library building complete the "culture square" of The Hague, which was intended to alleviate the rather sterile atmosphere of the neighboring ministries. Theaters by Herman Hertzberger and Rem Koolhaas are very close to the project, on the Turfmarkt and Spui sides, and projects designed by the architects Michael Graves, Cesar Pelli, and KPF planned

Diese sehr große Gebäudegruppe liegt in der Nähe des Hauptbahnhofs von Den Haag und in der Nachbarschaft des Justiz- und Außenministeriums auf einem schwierigen keilförmigen Gelände. Alle Bauten sind innen und außen mit weißen, 85 x 180 cm großen porzellan-emaillierten Metallplatten verkleidet. Der Straßenraster und das Grundstück inspirierten Meier dazu, eine zwölfgeschossige Büroscheibe und einen zehngeschossigen Block um 12,5° gegeneinander zu verschwenken. Dazwischen plazierte er das spektakulärste Element des Komplexes, ein 47 m hohes verglastes Atrium, das der größte Raum dieser Art in Europa sein wird. Rathaus und Bibliothek komplettieren den »Kulturplatz« Den Haags, der die sterile Atmosphäre der benachbarten Ministerien auflockern soll. Ganz in der Nähe, an den Seiten zu Turfmarkt und Spui, liegen die Theater von Herman Hertzberger und Rem Koolhaas. Für andere nahegelegene Grundstücke liegen Entwürfe der Architekten Michael Graves,

Recouverte à l'intérieur et à l'extérieur de panneaux en métal émaillé blanc de 85 x 180 cm, cette vaste réalisation se trouve près de la gare Centraal de La Haye, non loin des ministères de la Justice et des Affaires étrangères, sur un site de forme angulaire très difficile. S'inspirant de l'alignement des rues et du site, Meier opta pour une rotation de 12,5° des deux grilles principales de la structure, ce qui correspond dans le projet à la barre de bureaux de 12 étages et au bloc horizontal de 10 étages. Entre ces deux éléments, il a placé ce qu'il y a de plus extraordinaire dans la construction, un immense atrium vitré de 47 m de haut qui n'aura pas son pareil en Europe. L'hôtel de ville et la bibliothèque publique complètent le «Carré culturel» de la ville de La Haye conçu en vue d'atténuer l'atmosphère stérile et endormie de ce quartier de ministères. Les théâtres construits par Herman Hertzberger et Rem Koolhaas sont proches de ce complexe, sur le Turfmarkt et le Spui, et d'autres projets

for other nearby sites. The choice of Richard Meier was in fact the result of a limited competition between contractors. The client is technically not the city, but the ABP Pension Fund which have leased the site on a long-term basis from the central government. Three times the size of the Canal+ building in Paris, the project is being carried out with a nearly identical budget. Although it may not be possible to finish the City Hall in as fine a way as the KNP-BT building for example, Meier aims here to set a new standard of architectural quality for inexpensive public buildings.

Cesar Pelli und KPF vor. Die Wahl Richard Meiers war im Grunde das Ergebnis eines begrenzten Wettbewerbs unter den Baufirmen. Bauherr im technischen Sinne ist nicht die Stadt, sondern der ABP-Pensionsfonds, der das Grundstück langfristig vom Staat gepachtet hat. Das Projekt hat den dreifachen Umfang von Canal+ in Paris, wurde aber mit einem ungefähr gleich großen Budget durchgeführt. Obwohl das Rathaus wohl nicht so großzügig ausgestattet werden kann wie etwa das KNP-BT-Gebäude, bemühte sich Meier, einen neuen Standard architektonischer Qualität für kostengünstige öffentliche Bauten zu setzen.

dessinés par les architectes Michael Graves et César Pelli et par KPF sont prévus sur des sites voisins. Meier a été choisi comme architecte de ce projet après une simple consultation entre entrepreneurs. Le client n'est pas la ville mais les assurances vieillesse ABP qui ont loué le site au gouvernement par un bail à long terme. Trois fois de la taille de Canal+ à Paris, le projet a cependant été réalisé avec un budget à peu près équivalent. Bien qu'une aussi belle finition que celle de l'immeuble de KNP-BT, par exemple, ne s'avère pas possible financièrement dans ce complexe de La Haye, Richard Meier cherche ici à renouveler la qualité du vocabulaire formel et plastique de l'architecture publique d'un budget limité.

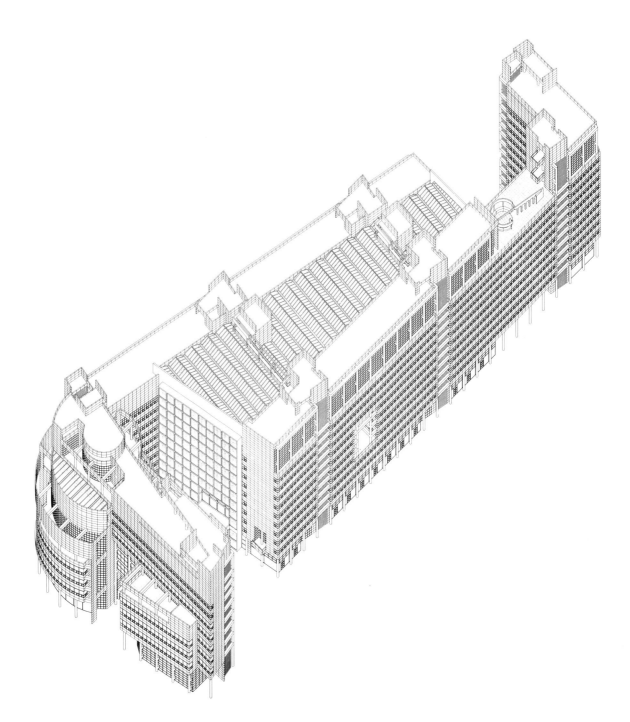

The most spectacular space of the complex is the glass-covered atrium, with its two banks of suspended bridges. The axonometric view reveals the curved volume of the library on the Spui side. The triangular atrium is formed by the 12,5° angle separating the two main blocks.

Der spektakulärste Raum des Komplexes ist das verglaste Atrium mit seinen zwei frei in den Raum gestellten Brückenkonstruktionen. Die Axonometrie zeigt das gekurvte Volumen der Bibliothek auf der Spui-Seite. Das dreieckige Atrium ist durch den Winkel von 12,50°, der die beiden Hauptblöcke trennt, entstanden.

L'atrium en verre avec ses deux travées de ponts suspendus est l'espace le plus spectaculaire de ce complexe. La vue axionométrique montre le volume courbe de la bibliothèque du côté du Spui. L'atrium triangulaire est formé par l'angle de 12,5° qui sépare les deux parties principales du complexe.

Weishaupt Forum

Schwendi, Germany
1988–1992

Located 30 km from Ulm, Schwendi has been the location of Max Weishaupt GmbH, which today builds gas burners, for 200 years. The Weishaupt Forum is a two-story gateway complex for their factory. It includes exhibition spaces for the products and a surprisingly good collection of postwar art, a 50-seat lecture hall, a cafeteria for 260 persons, a training center and offices. The total usable floor space is 5,200 m². It seems obvious that the present director of the firm, Siegfried Weishaupt, has a great interest in design. The extreme precision of the respect for the one meter grid in this building is one of its outstanding features, as is the remarkable play of light.

Schwendi liegt 30 km von Ulm entfernt und ist Sitz der Firma Max Weishaupt GmbH, die seit 200 Jahren Brenner herstellt. Das Weishaupt Forum ist ein zweigeschossiger »Tor«-Komplex für die Fabrik. Er enthält Ausstellungsbereiche für die Brenner und eine überraschend gute Sammlung von Nachkriegskunst, einen Vortragsraum für 50 Personen, eine Cafeteria für 260 Mitarbeiter, ein Schulungszentrum und Büros. Die gesamte Nutzfläche beträgt 5 200 m². Siegfried Weishaupt, der jetzige Direktor der Firma, ist offenbar sehr an Architektur und Design interessiert. Besondere Merkmale dieses Gebäudes sind seine extreme Präzision, der strenge Raster von 1 m und das Wechselspiel des Lichts in den offenen Räumen.

Schwendi, petite commune située à 30 km d'Ulm, est le siège de l'entreprise Max Weishaupt GmbH, fabricant de brûleurs à gaz depuis 200 ans. Le Weishaupt Forum est un complexe de deux étages qui sert d'accès à l'usine proprement dite. Il comprend des espaces d'exposition pour les brûleurs et une collection d'art d'après-guerre, un amphithéâtre de 50 places, un restaurant pour les 260 employés de l'entreprise, un centre de formation et des bureaux. En tout, la surface au sol est de 5 200 m². L'actuel P.D.G, Siegfried Weishaupt, manifeste un intérêt particulier pour l'architecture.

Pages 116/117: architecturally less elaborate than the KNP-BT headquarters, the Weishaupt Forum nonetheless places great emphasis on the quality of the construction. An evening view reveals the transparency of the exhibition gallery.

Seite 116/117: Das Weishaupt Forum ist architektonisch weniger ausgefeilt als die Hauptverwaltung der KNP-BT, legt aber großen Wert auf die Qualität der Konstruktion. Die Nachtansicht zeugt von der Transparenz des Ausstellungsbereichs.

Pages 116/117: d'une architecture moins élaborée que le siège des Papeteries Royales des Pays-Bas, le Weishaupt Forum fait preuve néanmoins d'une grande qualité de construction. Une vue le soir révèle la transparence de la galerie d'exposition.

"As has been said so many times, architecture can be thought of as frozen music, and the architect, then, as both the composer and the conductor. With Siegfried Weishaupt we have created a beautiful symphony at the Weishaupt Forum and one that will play on the mind's eye, I hope, for many years to come."

»Wie schon so oft gesagt wurde, kann man sich Architektur als gefrorene Musik denken und den Architekten als Komponisten wie als Dirigenten. Mit Siegfried Weishaupt haben wir im Weishaupt Forum eine schöne Symphonie geschaffen, die hoffentlich noch jahrelang das geistige Auge erfreuen wird.«

«Ainsi qu'il a été dit tant de fois, on peut imaginer l'architecture comme de la musique figée et l'architecte comme étant à la fois le compositeur et le chef d'orchestre. Siegfried Weishaupt et moi, nous avons créé une magnifique symphonie avec le Weishaupt Forum, qui jouera sur la prunelle de notre imagination, je l'espère, pour longtemps.»

Page 118 and above: a covered bridge connects the display/ reception area to the structure containing the company cafeteria. The reduced complexity of the geometry makes this a particularly successful building.
Pages 120/121: as in the Daimler-Benz Research Center in Ulm, the Weishaupt Forum houses the cafeteria in a circular volume.

Seite 118 und oben: Eine überdeckte Brücke verbindet den Ausstellungs- und Empfangsbereich mit der Cafeteria. Der Erfolg des Gebäudes beruht vor allem auf seiner reduzierten, komplexen Geometrie.
Seite 120/121: Wie beim Daimler-Benz Forschungszentrum in Ulm ist die Cafeteria des Weishaupt Forums in einem kreisförmigen Gebäude untergebracht.

Page 118 et ci-dessus: un pont couvert joint l'aire d'exposition et de réception à l'espace abritant la cafétéria. Cet édifice est particulièrement réussi grâce à sa géométrie d'une complexité réduite.
Pages 120/121: au Weishaupt Forum, à l'instar du centre de recherches Daimler-Benz à Ulm, le volume circulaire est affecté à la cafétéria.

Canal+ Headquarters

Paris, France
1988–1992

"I like to think of this building as Parisian in feeling," says Richard Meier, "intellectual yet sensual, and beautiful in its rationality. Spatially it is simple, but technically it is complex. The building's sheer wall becomes the placard both for Canal+ and its urban presence. Its image from the Seine is of a great ship whose only movement is the changing light." The headquarters of one of the most successful cable television companies in the world, this building is located in the 15th arrondissement, adjacent to the new André-Citroën Park, and also near to a good number of undistinguished modern office and residential buildings. Built on a very tight schedule between April 1990 and the end

»Ich denke mir dieses Gebäude gern als pariserisch«, sagt Richard Meier, »intellektuell und doch sinnlich und schön in seiner Rationalität. Räumlich ist es einfach, aber technisch ist es komplex. Die glatte Wand des Gebäudes wird zum Plakat für Canal+ und für seine urbane Präsenz. Von der Seine her sieht es aus wie ein großes Schiff, dessen einzige Bewegung im Wechsel des Lichts besteht.«
Die Hauptverwaltung für eine der erfolgreichsten Kabelfernsehgesellschaften der Welt liegt im 15. Arrondissement in der Nähe des neuen Parc André-Citroën, umgeben von mittelmäßigen modernen Büro- und Wohngebäuden. Das Gebäude entstand innerhalb eines sehr knappen Zeit-

«J'aime à penser que cette construction est parisienne dans l'âme, intellectuelle mais sensuelle, belle aussi dans sa rationalité. Simple sur le plan spatial mais complexe sur le plan technique. Le mur de l'édifice devient à lui seul l'enseigne de Canal+ et de sa présence urbaine. Vu de la Seine, on dirait un grand bateau dont l'unique mouvement serait celui de la lumière changeante.» Siège de l'une des télévisions câblées les plus prospères du monde, cet édifice a été construit dans le 15e arrondissement de Paris, non loin du parc André-Citroën, mais aussi de nombreux immeubles résidentiels et de bureaux d'un modernisme manquant de distinction. Bâti dans des dé-

Pages 122/123: as seen from the André-Citroën park, the Canal+ building is a thin volume inserted into a rather unattractive urban environment. The clean modernity of the building represents an appropriate symbol for this forward-looking private cable television operator.

Pages 124/125: the roof landscape of the Canal+ building offers some idea of the internal function of the structure – from the satellite dishes to the conical volume of a small screening room. The articulation of the facade confirms Meier's taste for a certain geometric complexity.

Seite 122/123: Vom Parc André-Citroën her gesehen wirkt das Gebäude von Canal+ wie eine schmale Scheibe, die sich in eine relativ unattraktive städtische Umgebung einfügt. Die klare Modernität des Gebäudes ist ein angemessenes Symbol für diesen progressiven privaten Kabelfernsehkanal.

Seite 124/125: Die Dachlandschaft von Canal+ macht die inneren Funktionen des Gebäudes deutlich – von den Satellitenschüsseln bis zum konischen Volumen eines kleinen Projektionsraumes. An der Fassadengliederung läßt sich Meiers Vorliebe für eine gewisse geometrische Komplexität ablesen.

Pages 122/123: vu du parc André-Citroën, l'édifice de Canal+ est un mince volume inséré dans un environnement urbain peu séduisant. La pure modernité du bâtiment est le symbole adéquat de cette chaîne de télévision par câble tournée vers les possibilités de l'avenir.

Pages 124/125: le toit de Canal+, pareil à un paysage, donne une idée de la fonction interne de la structure – des antennes paraboliques au volume conique d'une petite salle de projection. L'articulation structurelle de la façade confirme le goût de Meier pour une certaine complexité géométrique.

of 1991, the building has some 22,000 m² of usable space. Three four-story television studios, whose interiors Richard Meier was not called on to design, determined the form of the block on the eastern side, and there were severe site restrictions, such as differing height requirements. Light is omnipresent in this inspiring structure. With the large parabolic antennas on its roof, the Canal+ building projects just the sort of forward-looking image which the former director of the firm, André Rousselet wanted.

rahmens zwischen April 1990 und Ende 1991 und verfügt über eine Nutzfläche von etwa 22 000 m². Drei viergeschossige Fernsehstudios, die nicht zu Meiers Bauauftrag gehörten, bestimmten die Form des Blocks an der Ostseite. Strenge Bauvorschriften verlangten unterschiedliche Höhen. Im Inneren des Gebäudes ist Licht allgegenwärtig. Mit den großen Parabolantennen auf dem Dach übermittelt die Hauptverwaltung von Canal+ genau jenes progressive Image, das sich André Rousselet, der frühere Direktor, gewünscht hatte.

lais extrêmement courts, entre avril 1990 et décembre 1991, l'édifice a quelque 22 000 m² de surface au sol. La forme du bloc côté Est est entièrement déduite des trois studios de télévision hauts de quatre étages, que Meier n'a pas dessinés d'ailleurs. L'architecte dut faire face à diverses contraintes d'urbanisme pesant sur le site comme l'obligation de varier les hauteurs. La lumière est omniprésente dans cette belle structure qui inspire.

Page 126 and above: the sweeping terrace facing out toward the Seine recalls the architect's recurring use of nautical metaphors, but in this case, the ship seems as close to "Star Wars" as it does to Le Corbusier.

Seite 126 und oben: Die geschwungene Terrasse zur Seine hin zeigt wiederum die maritimen Metaphern des Architekten. Doch in diesem Fall ist das Schiff den »Star Wars« ebenso verwandt wie Le Corbusier.

Page 126 et ci-dessus: la longue terrasse cintrée donnant sur la Seine rappelle les métaphores navales, thème récurrent de Meier, mais ici le bateau est plus près de la «Guerre des étoiles» que de Le Corbusier.

"What makes my buildings American, even when they are built in Europe? There's a certain openness, a certain transparency, a certain lightness that is American. There is also the relationship between the building and nature, which may be more American, but I'm also interested in the kind of permanence and specificity which is European."

»Was macht meine Bauten amerikanisch, selbst wenn sie in Europa errichtet werden? Es gibt eine gewisse Offenheit, eine gewisse Transparenz, eine gewisse Leichtigkeit, die amerikanisch ist. Es gibt auch die Beziehung zum Grundstück, die Beziehung zwischen Gebäude und Natur, die vielleicht eher amerikanisch ist, aber ich interessiere mich auch für die Permanenz und Spezifität, die europäisch sind.«

«En quoi mes constructions sont américaines, même si elles sont réalisées en Europe? Elles ont quelque chose d'ouvert, de transparent, de clair, qui est américain. Il y a aussi le rapport au site, le rapport entre la construction et la nature qui sont peut-être plus américains, mais je m'intéresse également à la permanence et à la spécificité, qui sont européennes.»

Pages 128/129: the boardroom with desk and lighting designed by Meier, a rear facade, and the spectacular entrance lobby with its rough Vosges granite floors.

Seite 128/129: Der Sitzungssaal mit Tisch und Beleuchtung nach Meiers Entwurf, Ansicht der Rückseite und die spektakuläre Eingangshalle mit ihrem Boden aus rauhem Vogesengranit.

Pages 128/129: la salle de conférences avec le bureau et l'éclairage dessinés par Meier, une façade arrière et le hall d'entrée impressionnant avec son sol en granite brut des Vosges.

"There are very different kinds of spaces in the Canal+ Head-quarters, the studio spaces and the production spaces have different kinds of requirements in terms of light, space, scale, than the offices, so it seemed to appropriate to divide the areas accordingly."

»Es gibt sehr unterschiedliche Arten von Räumen in der Canal+ Hauptverwaltung: die Studioräume und die Produktionsräume haben in Licht, Größe, Maßstab völlig andere Anforderungen als die Büroräume, deshalb schien es angebracht, das zum Ausdruck zu bringen.«

«Il y a des espaces de nature très différente à Canal+; les studios et l'unité de production ont en matière de lumière, d'espace et d'échelle des exigences différentes de celles des bureaux, aussi me semble-t-il justifié de diviser les espaces en fonction de ces différences.»

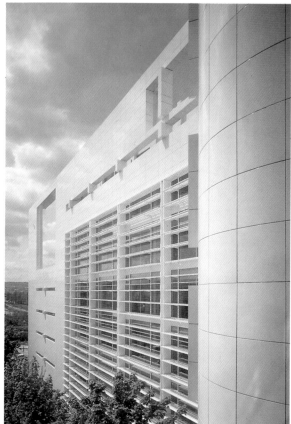

Exhibition and Assembly Building

Ulm, Germany
1986–1993

The Exhibition and Assembly Building in Ulm was dedicated on November 12, 1993. The 3,500 m² three-story complex clad in Rosa Dante granite and white stucco, without any metal panels, houses exhibition spaces, a large assembly hall, a café and a tourist information center. It is notable not only for its design, but also for the ways in which Richard Meier has resolved the complex problems posed by the site in the Münsterplatz, which he was also called upon to redesign. The historic center of this town with 100,000 inhabitants is dominated by the 161 meter tall Ulm Münster Cathedral. 85% of the historic city was destroyed by bombing in 1944, and the reconstruction of Ulm was carried out without much regard for the quality of the architecture. The curving, pedestrian Hirschstrasse leads from the train station to the square, where Meier has placed a curved wall which leads people into the square. A glass bridge with a pedestrian underpass links the two basic elements of the structure, facilitating the penetration of the space, as do the

Das Stadthaus in Ulm wurde am 12. November 1993 eingeweiht. Der 3 500 m² große, dreigeschossige Komplex ist mit Rosa Dante-Granit und weißem Putz verkleidet, diesmal ohne Verwendung von Emailplatten. Er beherbergt Ausstellungsräume, einen großen Saal, ein Café und das Verkehrsbüro. Bemerkenswert ist das Gebäude nicht nur wegen seiner eigenen Architektur, sondern auch wegen Meiers Umgang mit den komplexen Problemen des Münsterplatzes, für den er eine neue Pflasterung entwarf. Das historische Zentrum dieser Stadt von 100 000 Einwohnern wird von dem fast 161 m hohen Turm des Ulmer Münsters beherrscht. 1944 wurden 85% der Altstadt durch Bomben zerstört, und beim Wiederaufbau Ulms nahm man wenig Rücksicht auf architektonische Qualität. Die Fußgängerzone Hirschstraße führt vom Bahnhof zum Münsterplatz, wo Meier eine gekurvte Wand plazierte, die den Besucher zum Platz hin leitet. Eine Glasbrücke mit einer darunterliegenden Fußgängerpassage verbindet die beiden Baukörper und erleichtert den

Le complexe administratif et culturel de la ville d'Ulm a été inauguré le 12 novembre 1993. D'une superficie totale de 3 500 m², cet ensemble de trois étages, habillé de granit Rosa Dante et de stuc blanc sans la moindre utilisation de panneau en métal, comprend des espaces d'exposition, une grande salle de réunion, un café-restaurant et un office de tourisme. Ce qui est remarquable dans cet édifice, ce n'est pas seulement son plan mais aussi les réponses trouvées par l'architecte aux difficiles problèmes posés par le site, la Münsterplatz, que Meier fut d'ailleurs chargé de redessiner. Le centre historique de cette ville de 100 000 habitants est dominé par la flèche de la cathédrale Münster, haute de 161 mètres. Les bombardements de 1944 avaient détruit 85% du vieux quartier qu'on avait reconstruit ensuite sans se soucier beaucoup de la qualité architecturale de l'ensemble. La Hirschstrasse, curviligne et piétonne, part de la grande gare pour aboutir à la place où Meier a placé un mur courbe qui conduit les passants jusque sur le parvis. Un pont

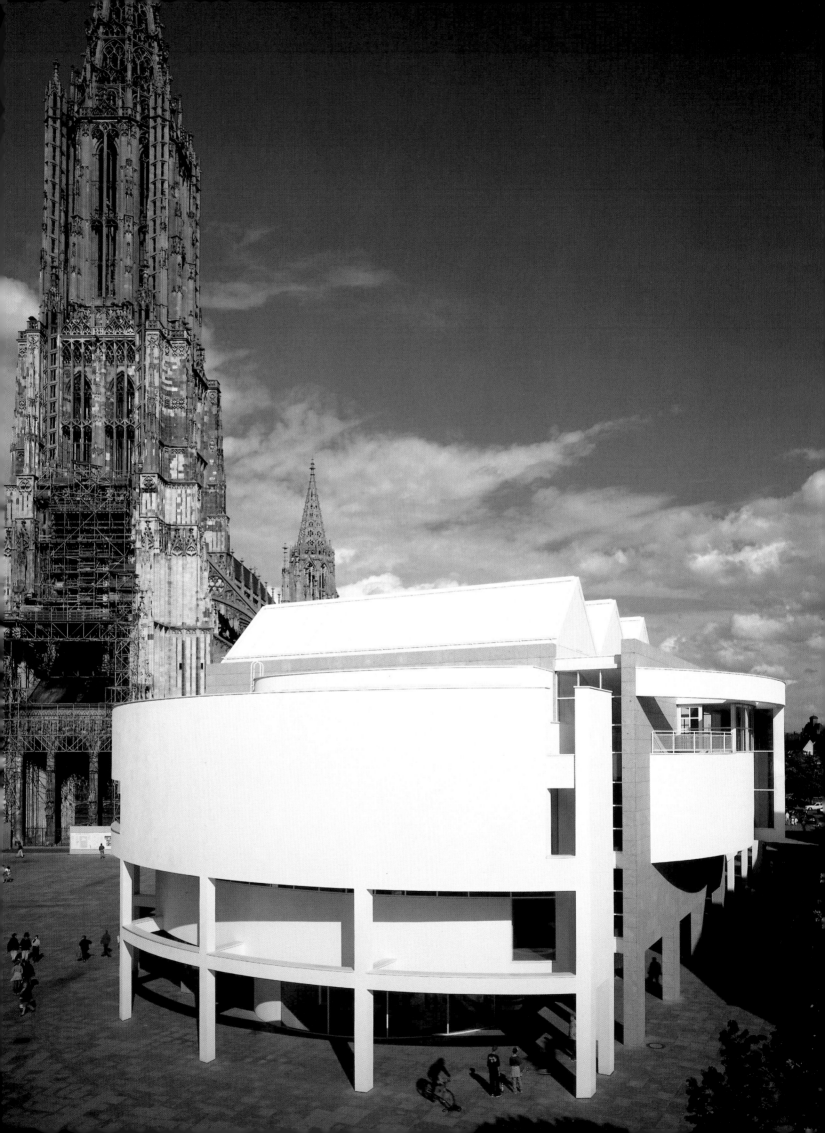

numerous possible points of
entry into the building itself.
As Meier points out, one of
the interesting features of the
building is the proliferation of
points of view throughout the
building toward the cathedral
spire.

Zugang ebenso wie die zahlreichen Eingänge zum Haupt-
gebäude. Wie Meier selbst
betont, zählen die zahlreichen
Ausblicke auf den Münsterturm von innen her zu den
interessanten Merkmalen des
Gebäudes.

de verre complété par un
passage souterrain piétonnier
lie les deux structures de base
du complexe, ce qui permet de
pénétrer facilement dans
l'espace comme le permettent
aussi les nombreux points
d'entrée dans l'édifice lui-
même. Ainsi que l'a fait re-
marquer Meier, une des particularités de cette construction
se trouve à l'intérieur où se
multiplient les points de vue
sur la flèche de la cathédrale.

Daimler-Benz Research Center

Ulm, Germany
1989–1993

Richard Meier's master-plan for an eventual research campus, inspired by the University of Virginia, and eight times as large as this project will undoubtedly never be carried out due to the changes in the economic and political climate in Germany since 1989. As it is, the complex is close to the Ulm University, on a hill overlooking the city where Richard Meier has recently completed the Exhibition and Assembly Building. The appearance of the Daimler-Benz buildings is not improved by the mediocre neighboring AEG research building de-signed by an in-house architect. Then too, a gate-house built on Meier's plans but without his supervision, shows just how important perfect construction and carefully executed design is to his projects. A large curving cafeteria space and the extensive use of 180 x 70 cm aluminum panels mark these structures, as do the very large rear top-lit research labs, whose interiors, like the Canal+ studios, were not desi-gned by the architect. An amusing sidelight to this project is the fact that the client very much wanted Meier to

Richard Meiers Masterplan für eine »Wissenschaftsstadt«, von der University of Virginia inspiriert und achtmal so groß wie der dortige Campus, wird wahrscheinlich nie ausgeführt werden, weil sich das politische und ökonomische Klima in Deutschland seit 1989 verändert hat. Das Forschungszentrum liegt in der Nähe der Ulmer Universität auf einem Berg über der Stadt, in der Meier das Stadthaus errichtete. Das Erscheinungsbild der Daimler-Benz-Bauten wird beeinträchtigt durch die mittelmäßigen Bauten des AEG-Forschungsinstituts, die von einem Firmenarchitekten entworfen wurden. Zudem zeigt ein Eingangsgebäude, das nach Meiers Plänen, aber nicht unter seiner Aufsicht gebaut wurde, wie wichtig bei seinen Projekten perfekte Konstruktion und sorgfältige Ausführung sind. Charakteristisch für den Komplex sind die Rotunde des »Kommunikationsgebäudes« und die 180 x 70 cm großen Alupaneele ebenso wie die sehr großen, durch Oberlichter erhellten Forschungslabors, deren Innenräume wie die Studios von Canal+ nicht von

Il est peu probable que le plan d'ensemble d'un vaste complexe de recherche universitaire inspiré du campus de l'université de Virginia et huit fois de la taille du projet Daimler-Benz soit jamais réalisé, vu l'évolution économique et politique en Allemagne depuis 1989. Le centre Daimler-Benz se trouve près de l'université d'Ulm, sur une hauteur dominant la ville où récemment encore Richard Meier achevait la construction du centre administratif et culturel. L'apparence générale des bâtiments n'est pas rehaussée par la médiocrité du centre de recherche AEG voisin dessiné par un architecte de la firme. En outre, une maison servant d'accès, construite sur les plans de Meier mais sans son contrôle, montre combien une construction parfaite et une exécution soignée du dessin sont importantes pour ses projets. C'est le grand espace circulaire réservé à la cafétéria et l'utilisation extensive de panneaux en métal de format 180 x 70 cm qui caractérisent ces structures, de même que les laboratoires éclairés par un vitrage dans la toiture et dont

use color inside the buildings. A single hallway, in which one side of each office entrance is painted in a subtle shade of blue or green, is all that remains of this request, which the client abandoned because of the difficulty of providing adequate maintenance.

Meier entworfen wurden. Amüsant ist die Tatsache, daß der Bauherr sich von Meier die Verwendung von Farben im Inneren wünschte. Von diesem Wunsch, der wegen der schwierigen Instandhaltung aufgegeben werden mußte, ist nur ein einziger Korridor übriggeblieben, in dem eine Seite von jedem Büroeingang zartblau oder -grün gestrichen ist.

l'intérieur, comme les studios de Canal+, n'a pas été réalisé par Meier. Une anecdote assez amusante sur le projet est éloquente: le client tenait beaucoup à ce que Meier mette de la couleur à l'intérieur des bâtiments. Tout ce qui subsiste de cette requête, que le client dut abandonner en raison des difficultés à assurer un entretien adéquat, est un couloir où chaque entrée de bureaux est peinte d'un côté dans une légère teinte de bleu ou de vert.

Pages 136/137: Richard Meier had intended to place a large sculpture in the basin near the building containing the cafeteria, but his suggestion that Frank Stella be called on was rejected.
Page 139: the curved volume visible to the right contains the corporate dining facilities, and the rectangular blocks to the rear, the research laboratories.

Seite 136/137: Richard Meier wollte ursprünglich eine große Skulptur in dem Becken nahe der Cafeteria aufstellen, doch sein Vorschlag, sich an Frank Stella zu wenden, wurde abgelehnt.
Seite 139: Der gekurvte Bau rechts enthält die Kantine und die rechteckigen Blocks im Hintergrund die Forschungslabors.

Pages 136/137: Richard Meier aurait aimé placer une grande sculpture dans le bassin qui se trouve près du bâtiment de la cafétéria, mais la direction rejeta son idée de faire appel pour cela à Frank Stella.
Page 139: le volume arrondi qu'on peut voir sur la droite abrite le restaurant de l'entreprise, et les bâtiments rectangulaires se trouvant derrière, les laboratoires de recherche.

National Library of France

Paris, France
1989

Richard Meier was undoubtedly quite disappointed that his project for this very large library was not considered more seriously before the young French architect Dominique Perrault was chosen. Indeed the long main structure would surely have functioned better as a library than the four one hundred meter high towers designed by the Frenchman. The monumental reading room facing the Seine was certainly a reference to Labrouste's 1868 Bibliothèque Nationale room, proving once again that Meier makes constant, indirect references to the history of architecture. The six-story main library stacks "are divided into five reference sections according to specific categories". Perrault's project with its towers seems to have provided the signal of recognition which the French government organizers of the competition were seeking, but Richard Meier's project also included an immediately recognizable tower.

Richard Meier war zweifellos sehr enttäuscht darüber, daß sein Projekt für diese sehr große Bibliothek nicht ernsthafter in Betracht gezogen wurde, bevor der junge französische Architekt Dominique Perrault den Wettbewerb gewann. Tatsächlich wäre der lange Hauptbau bestimmt besser als Bibliothek geeignet gewesen als die vier einhundert Meter hohen Türme Perraults. Der monumentale Lesesaal zur Seine hin bezog sich sicherlich auf den von Labrouste in der Nationalbibliothek (1868) – ein weiterer Beweis dafür, daß Meier ständig indirekte Verbindungen zur Architekturgeschichte herstellt. Das sechsgeschossige Hauptdepot ist »nach bestimmten Kriterien in fünf Fachbereiche unterteilt«. Perraults Projekt mit seinen Türmen lieferte zwar ein Erkennungszeichen, wie es die Vertreter des französischen Staates, die den Wettbewerb organisiert hatten, suchten; aber auch Meiers Entwurf wartete mit einem direkt erkennbaren Turm auf.

Ce fut une grande déception pour Richard Meier de ne pas voir son projet plus sérieusement examiné avant que celui du jeune architecte français Dominique Perrault ait été choisi. C'est un fait que la structure principale toute en longueur se serait mieux prêtée au fonctionnement d'une bibliothèque que les quatre tours de cent mètres de haut dessinées par le Français. Avec sa grande salle de lecture face à la Seine, Meier faisait très certainement référence à celle de la Bibliothèque Nationale construite par Labrouste en 1868, preuve une fois de plus qu'il ne cesse de se référer indirectement à l'histoire de l'architecture. Les galeries organisées sur six niveaux «sont divisées en cinq unités d'ouvrages de consultation classés par catégories spécifiques». Les quatre tours du projet de Perrault semblent avoir représenté l'emblème visible de la bibliothèque que souhaitait le gouvernement français, même si, dans son projet, Meier avait présenté lui aussi une tour signalant la présence de la bibliothèque.

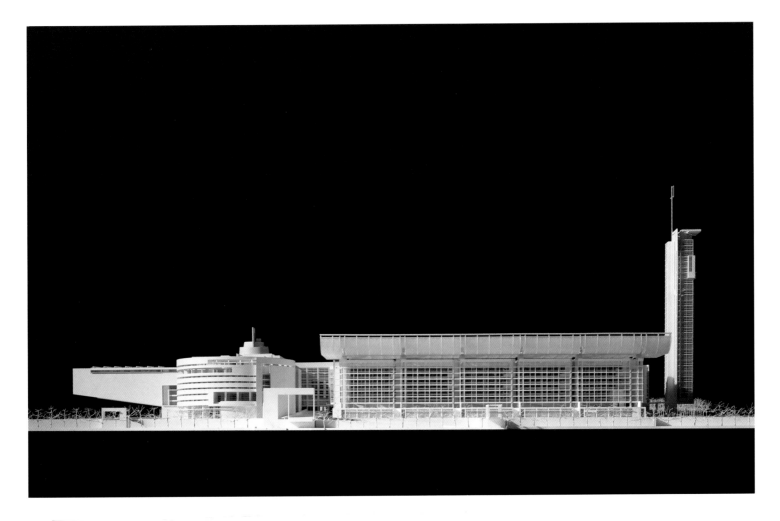

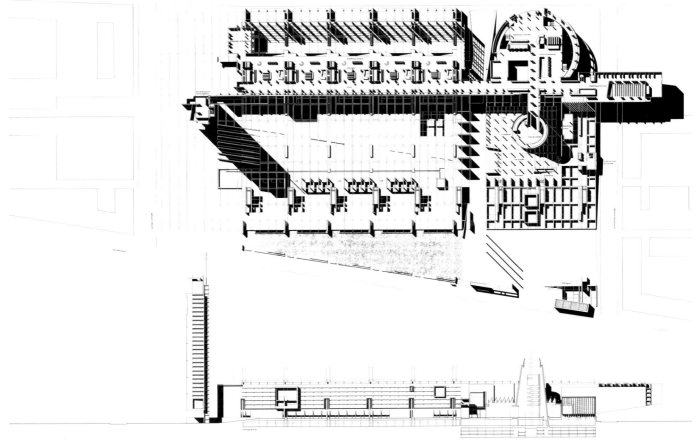

Sextius-Mirabeau Master Plan

Aix-en-Provence, France
1990

This plan for the redevelopment of an industrial area in Aix-en-Provence, a southern French city with a very rich history, was not carried out. It was designed to extend the tree-lined Cours Mirabeau, which Meier calls the "linear center of the city". Including residential, commercial and cultural facilities, the plan called for a convention center, a casino/hotel and a rail and bus station. Although it is a coincidence related to the area to be developed, this project, like the Berlin housing plan, adopts a long curvilinear form.

Dieser Plan für die Sanierung eines Industriegebiets in Aix-en-Provence, einer südfranzösischen Stadt mit sehr reicher Geschichte, wurde nicht realisiert. Er sollte den baumgesäumten Cours Mirabeau weiterführen, den Meier »das lineare Zentrum der Stadt« nennt. Außer Wohn-, Geschäfts- und Kulturbauten sah der Plan ein Kongreßzentrum, ein Kasino/ Hotel sowie eine Bahn- und Busstation vor. Obwohl es ein Zufall ist, der mit dem Sanierungsgebiet zusammenhängt, hat auch dieses Projekt wie die Berliner Wohnbebauung eine langgestreckte gekurvte Form.

La rénovation d'un quartier industriel d'Aix-en-Provence, ville du midi de la France, est restée un projet de papier. Le plan prévoyait le prolongement du cours Mirabeau bordé d'arbres, que Richard Meier nomme le «centre linéaire de la ville.» Le projet comprenait des installations culturelles, commerciales et résidentielles, mais prévoyait aussi la construction d'un palais des congrès, d'un hôtel casino et d'une gare routière et ferroviaire. Pure coïncidence due à la zone à rénover, ce projet adopte, à l'instar du projet de logements de Berlin, une longue forme curviligne.

Hypolux Bank Building

Luxembourg
1990–1993

The business of banking in Luxembourg has been thriving, as evidenced by the new Bank of Luxembourg headquarters in the center of the city, designed by the Florida firm Arquitectonica, and the 1991 Gottfried Böhm building for the Deutsche Bank, which is located near Meier's site, on the outskirts of the city. Meier was chosen by competition. There is a large cylindrical volume with a trademark four-story atrium, and an office "slab", the whole designed around a 90 cm module. Unlike Daimler-Benz, which did not accede to the architect's suggestion that a Frank Stella sculpture be placed in the center of the Ulm complex, there is one here, in the plaza in front of the building.

Das Bankgeschäft in Luxemburg steht in voller Blüte, wie es die neue Hauptverwaltung der Bank von Luxemburg im Zentrum der Stadt, entworfen von der Firma Arquitectonica aus Florida, und Gottfried Böhms Gebäude der Deutschen Bank von 1991 beweisen. Böhms Bank liegt in der Nähe von Meiers Grundstück am Rande der Stadt. Meier war Gewinner des Wettbewerbs. Der Komplex besteht aus einem großen zylindrischen Volumen mit einem charakteristischen, vier Geschosse hohen Atrium und einer Büroscheibe, alles nach einem Modul von 90 cm geplant. Anders als bei Daimler-Benz, wo man nicht auf den Wunsch des Architekten einging, eine Skulptur von Frank Stella in die Mitte des Ulmer Komplexes zu plazieren, steht hier ein Werk von Stella auf dem Platz vor dem Gebäude.

Les affaires bancaires ont beaucoup prospéré au Luxembourg, comme en témoignent le nouveau siège de la Banque du Luxembourg dessiné par Arquitectonica, une agence de Floride, et l'immeuble de la Deutsche Bank conçu par l'architecte Gottfried Böhm en 1991, situé non loin de la banque Hypolux, dans la banlieue de la ville. Meier fut choisi par concours. Son projet comprend un grand volume cylindrique renfermant un atrium d'une hauteur de quatre étages, qui représente en quelque sorte la marque de fabrique de l'architecte, et un bloc de bureaux, le tout étant conçu à partir d'un module de 90 cm de côté. Sur la place devant la banque est exposée une œuvre de Frank Stella.

Pages 144/145: like Canal+ this client undoubtedly chose Richard Meier in order to underline its progressive reputation. A plan emphasizing a circle and squares seems typical of the architect, as does the use of complex "brise soleils."
Pages 146/147: certainly more appropriate for the architecture than the sculpture chosen by Daimler-Benz, here, a work by Frank Stella completes the composition.

Seite 144/145: Wie Canal+ wählte auch dieser Bauherr zweifellos Richard Meier, um seinen progressiven Ruf zu betonen. Der Grundriß aus einem Kreis und Quadraten ist ebenso typisch für den Architekten wie die Verwendung komplexer »Brisesoleils«.
Seite 146/147: Hier vollendet ein Werk Frank Stellas die Komposition, das der Architektur sicherlich angemessener ist als die von Daimler-Benz gewählte Skulptur.

Pages 144/145: le client de ce projet, comme celui de Canal+, choisit de faire appel à Richard Meier très certainement pour mettre en avant sa réputation de banque progressiste. Le plan faisant bien ressortir cercle et carré est typique de l'architecte, de même que l'utilisation de brise-soleil complexes.
Pages 146/147: une œuvre de Frank Stella, convenant certainement mieux à l'architecture que la sculpture choisie par Daimler-Benz, termine la composition.

Page 148 and above: in almost all of his projects, Richard Meier has created high, open areas. Here an elegant spiral staircase punctuates the space.

Seite 148 und oben: Bei nahezu allen seinen Projekten schuf Richard Meier hohe, offene Bereiche. Hier akzentuiert eine elegante Wendeltreppe den Raum.

Page 148 et ci-dessus: Richard Meier a créé dans presque tous ses projets des espaces hauts et ouverts. Ici, il les a ponctués d'un élégant escalier circulaire.

Museum of Ethnology

Frankfurt/Main, Germany
1989

Another abandoned project which was to be situated near the Museumsufer, close to Meier's Museum for the Decorative Arts, this seems to be the unbuilt work which the architect regrets the most. Organized around a "long, glazed ramp hall", the museum was to house its African collection on the ground floor, works from the Americas on the second floor and Oceanic art above. Design challenges included the need to preserve as many trees as possible on the site and to place large displays such as boats and a clay Masai hut.

Daß dieses Projekt aufgegeben wurde, das am Museumsufer nahe Meiers Museum für Kunsthandwerk entstehen sollte, bedauerte der Architekt wohl am meisten. Das Museum war um eine »lange, verglaste Rampenhalle« organisiert und sollte im Erdgeschoß die Afrikanische Sammlung, im ersten Obergeschoß die Amerikanische Sammlung und darüber die Ozeanische Kunst aufnehmen. Zu den Entwurfsbedingungen gehörte die Erhaltung von möglichst vielen Bäumen. Außerdem sollte das Museum Raum bieten für große Objekte wie Boote und eine Lehmhütte der Massai.

Cet autre projet est peut-être celui que Richard Meier regrette le plus de n'avoir pas pu réaliser. Il devait être situé près du Museumsufer et du musée des Arts décoratif construit par l'architecte. Organisé autour de la «longue rampe vitrée» de l'espace de réception, le musée devait présenter sa collection africaine au rez-de-chaussée, celle des Indiens d'Amérique au premier étage et celle d'Océanie tout en haut. Parmi les défis à relever, il y avait la préservation du plus grand nombre d'arbres possible sur le site et l'exposition de pièces aussi volumineuses que des bateaux et d'une case de terre sèche Masaï.

Museum of Contemporary Art

Barcelona, Spain
1987–1995

Richard Meier feels that this new museum will be one of his most successful projects. Located across the street from the Casa de la Caritat, the building includes a ramp leading to the main entry and to the three-story cylindrical reception area, with openings toward the large, flexible galleries. As Richard Meier tells the story, "At dinner one night in New York a few years ago I met Mayor Pasqual Maragall of Barcelona, who was the guest of honor. He asked me what type of building I would like to do in Barcelona. My answer was simple, a museum." Although not as difficult to finish as Gae Aulenti's Museu National d'Art de Catalunya, this Contemporary Art Museum did take a good deal of time from the first phase to completion. It is yet another element in the ongoing rivalry for Spanish cultural supremacy between Madrid and Barcelona.

Richard Meier glaubt, daß dieses neue Museum einer seiner gelungensten Bauten sein wird. Das Gebäude liegt gegenüber der Casa de la Caritat. Eine Rampe führt zum Haupteingang und zu dem drei Geschosse hohen zylindrischen Empfangsbereich, der sich auf die großen, flexiblen Ausstellungsräume öffnet. Meier erzählt: »Vor ein paar Jahren traf ich in New York beim Abendessen den Ehrengast, Bürgermeister Pasqual Maragall aus Barcelona. Er fragte mich, welche Art Gebäude ich gern für Barcelona bauen würde. Meine Antwort war einfach, ein Museum.« Obwohl es nicht so viele Schwierigkeiten bietet wie Gae Aulentis Museu National d'Art de Catalunya, braucht dieses Museum für Zeitgenössische Kunst von der ersten Phase bis zur Fertigstellung sehr viel Zeit.

Richard Meier a le sentiment que ce nouveau musée sera parmi les plus réussis de ses projets. Situé de l'autre côté de la rue de la Casa de la Caritat, l'édifice se compose d'une rampe menant à l'entrée principale et d'une aire de réception de forme cylindrique, à triple hauteur, s'ouvrant sur les vastes galeries conçues sur le principe de la flexibilité. Richard Meier raconte la naissance de ce projet: «Au cours d'un dîner à New York, il y a quelques années, je rencontrai le maire de Barcelone, Pasqual Maragall, qui était l'invité d'honneur. Il me demanda quel genre d'édifice il me plairait de construire à Barcelone. Ma réponse fut simple: un musée.» Bien que n'étant pas aussi difficile à finir que le Museu National d'Art de Catalunya de Gae Aulenti, la réalisation de ce musée d'art contemporain a nécessité tout de même beaucoup de temps, de sa première phase jusqu'à son achèvement.

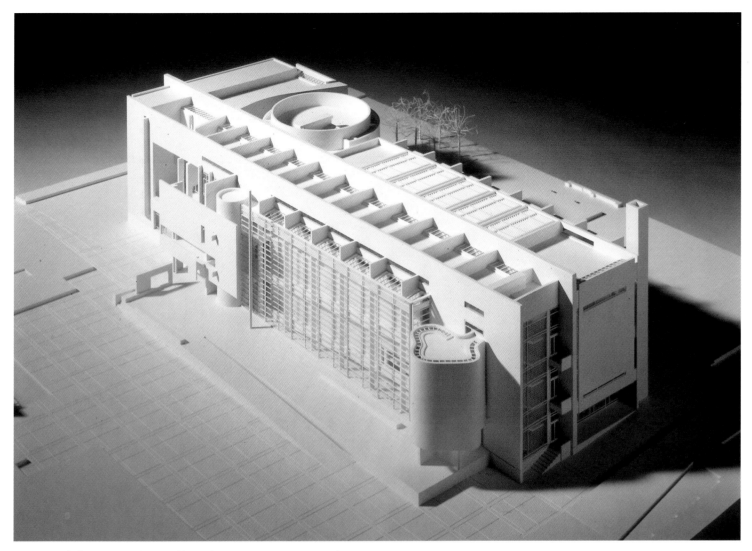

Page 152 and above: situated in the old city, this structure signals the manifestly modern nature of its contents, while maintaining a "low profile and contextual harmony".

Seite 152 und oben: Dieser Bau, in der Altstadt gelegen, demonstriert den modernen Charakter seines Inhalts und bewahrt zugleich »ein niedriges Profil und Harmonie mit der Umgebung«.

Page 152 et ci-dessus: bâti dans le cadre de la vieille ville de Barcelone, ce musée dévoile le caractère manifestement moderne de ce qu'il recèle tout en conservant «un profil bas et une harmonie de nature contextuelle».

Swissair North American Headquarters

Melville, New York
1990–1995

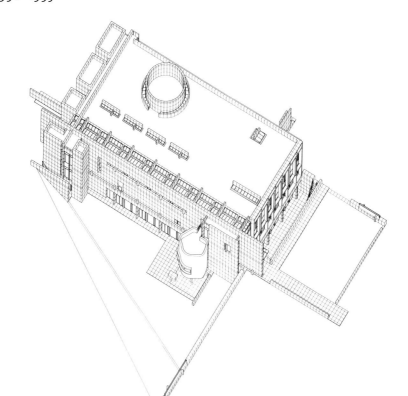

A frequent theme of Richard Meier's, the contrast between a closed and an open area is here given its impetus by the proximity of the very busy Long Island Expressway. There are two floors and a lower level, and two main entrances. There is a two-story reception area and atrium running along the entire building. On the second floor, there are open office and conference spaces, while part of the communications and computer facilities are located in the basement. As always, suffused with light, the Swissair headquarters should provide those who work there with a "pleasant and unique environment," as Meier's own documents indicate.

Ein häufiges Thema Richard Meiers, der Kontrast zwischen offenen und geschlossenen Bereichen, geht hier auf die Nähe des sehr verkehrsreichen Long Island Expressway zurück. Das Gebäude hat zwei Geschosse und ein Untergeschoß und verfügt über zwei Haupteingänge. Der Empfangsbereich, ein zwei Geschosse hohes Atrium, nimmt die gesamte Länge des Gebäudes ein. Im ersten Obergeschoß befinden sich offene Büro- und Konferenzräume, während die Kommunikations- und Computereinrichtungen teilweise im Untergeschoß untergebracht sind. Lichtdurchflutet wie alle Meier-Bauten, soll das Gebäude der Swissair allen dort Arbeitenden eine »angenehme und einzigartige Umgebung« bieten, wie der Architekt sagt.

Un des thèmes de prédilection de Richard Meier, le contraste entre espace ouvert et espace fermé, prend ici tout son sens grâce à la proximité de la Long Island Expressway, voie express très fréquentée. Cet édifice, qui a deux entrées principales, se compose de deux étages sur un niveau en soussol. Au premier étage se trouvent une aire de réception et un atrium d'une hauteur de deux étages occupant toute la longueur du bâtiment. Le second étage comprend des espaces de bureaux et de salles de conférence tandis que les installations informatiques et de télécommunications se trouvent partiellement au sous-sol. Etant toujours éclairé d'une lumière abondante, le siège de Swissair devrait représenter pour tous ceux qui y travaillent «un environnement unique et agréable», comme il est précisé dans le dossier du projet.

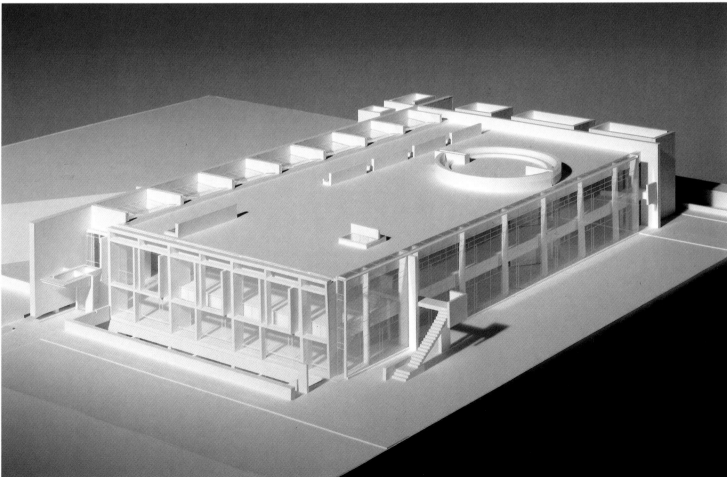

Getty Center

Los Angeles, California
1985–1997

The very figures give an impression of the size of this project. Its estimated cost is $733 million, with the site preparation alone costing $115 million. The new Getty Center will provide 87,800 m² of space, excluding entrance and parking facilities. The complex will cover 9,7 hectares of the 44,5 hectare site. An adjoining 243 hectares owned by the Getty Trust will preserve the natural quality of the area. In many respects, this is the largest project granted to a single architect in the late 20th century. And the first impressions of it confirm that it will mark the period in more ways than one. "In my mind's eye," Richard Meier has said, "I see a classic structure, elegant and timeless, emerging, serene and ideal, from the rough hillside, a kind of Aristotelian structure within the landscape. Sometimes I think that the landscape overtakes

Allein schon die Zahlen geben einen Eindruck von der Größe dieses Projekts. Die geschätzten Kosten betragen 733 Millionen Dollar, davon entfallen 115 Millionen Dollar auf die Grundstücksvorbereitung. Das neue Getty Center wird, ohne Eingangsgebäude und Parkplätze, 87 800 m² Raum bieten. Der Komplex bedeckt 9,7 Hektar des 44,5 Hektar großen Grundstücks. Eine angrenzende Fläche von 243 Hektar, die dem Getty Trust gehört, soll die natürliche Qualität der Umgebung erhalten. Dies ist in mancher Hinsicht das größte Projekt, das einem einzelnen Architekten im späten 20. Jahrhundert anvertraut wurde. Und die ersten Eindrücke bestätigen, daß es einen Markstein für diese Zeit setzen wird. »Vor meinem geistigen Auge«, sagte Meier, »sehe ich einen klassischen Bau, elegant und zeitlos, ruhig und vollkommen

Les chiffres à eux seuls donnent une idée de la monumentalité du projet. La réalisation est estimée globalement à 733 millions de dollars, la préparation du site coûtant à elle seule 115 millions. Le nouveau Getty Center couvrira une superficie totale de 87 800 m² sans compter l'aire d'accès et le parking. Le complexe occupera 9,7 hectares sur les quelque 44,5 hectares du site. Un terrain contigu de 243 hectares appartenant au Getty Trust permettra de protéger l'environnement sur le site. C'est à maints égards le plus grand projet culturel jamais réalisé par un seul architecte de toute cette période de fin de siècle. La première impression qu'on peut en avoir confirme l'idée que ce sera une borne milliaire de l'architecture moderne, et ce à plus d'un point de vue. «Je vois une structure classique, élé-

Pages 156/157: the only section of this very large complex, aside from restaurant facilities, which will be fully open to the public is the Museum, located near the tramway station.
Pages 158/159: the large circular volume on the left of this model, is the Center for the History of Art and the Humanities. The Museum is near the center of the model.

Seite 156/157: Abgesehen von den Restaurants ist der einzige total öffentliche Abschnitt dieses sehr großen Komplexes das Museum, das nahe der Bahnstation liegt.
Seite 158/159: Das große kreisförmige Volumen an der linken Seite dieses Modells ist das Center for the History of Art and the Humanities. Das Museum liegt nahe der Modell-Mitte.

Pages 156/157: le musée de cet immense complexe, situé près de la station de tramway, sera le seul avec le restaurant à être entièrement ouvert au public.
Pages 158/159: le vaste volume circulaire situé à gauche sur cette maquette représente le centre d'histoire de l'art et des sciences humaines. Le musée lui-même se trouve vers le centre de l'ensemble architectural.

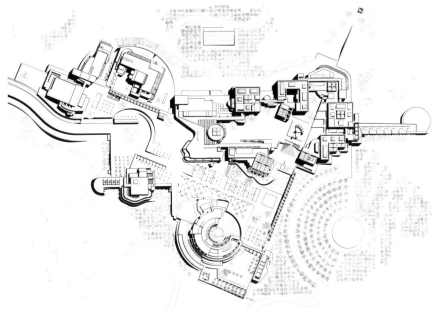

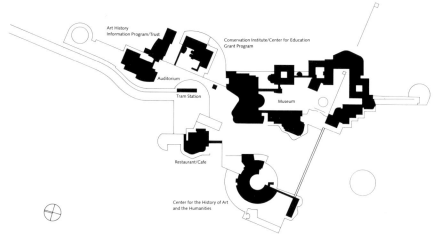

it, and sometime I see the structure as standing out, dominating the landscape; The two are entwined in a dialogue, a perpetual embrace in which building and site are one. In my mind I keep returning to the Romans – to Hadrian's Villa, to Caprarola – for their sequence of spaces, their thick-walled presence, their sense of order, the way in which building and landscape belong to each other".
Set on a dramatic hilltop site above the San Diego Freeway, the Getty already stands out like a fortress or a monastery above Los Angeles. This is in part due to the vast retaining walls clad in cleft travertine. This Italian stone strikes an entirely new note in the architecture of Richard Meier, and highlights the deep connections which his architecture has always had to the monuments of the past. Various forms of local opposition obliged the architect to abandon his trademark white surfaces. Even the metal panels used here will have a light beige tone. Although he insists on the "Italian hill town" aspect of the design, the complex as it is being built does have a rather remote appearance, which is clearly alleviated as the visitor reaches the esplanade in front of the museum.

aus dem rauhen Hügel hervortretend, eine aristotelische Struktur in der Landschaft. Manchmal denke ich, die Landschaft überwältigt sie, und manchmal sehe ich, wie die Struktur hervortritt und ihrerseits die Landschaft beherrscht. Beide sind in einen Dialog verwickelt, eine ständige Umarmung, in der Bauwerk und Umgebung eins werden. Im Geiste kehre ich immer wieder zu den Römern zurück – zur Hadriansvilla, nach Caprarola – wegen ihrer Raumfolgen, ihrer dickwandigen Präsenz, ihrem Sinn für Ordnung, wegen der Art, wie Bauwerk und Landschaft sich miteinander verbinden.« Das Getty Center in seiner dramatischen Hügellage über dem San Diego Freeway wirkt bereits wie eine Festung oder ein Kloster oberhalb von Los Angeles. Das liegt teilweise an den riesigen Stützmauern, die mit gespaltenem Travertin verkleidet sind. Dieser italienische Stein schlägt eine völlig neue Note in Meiers Architektur an. Lokale Opposition zwang den Architekten, auf seine charakteristischen weißen Flächen zu verzichten. Selbst die Metallplatten werden hier einen hellbeigen Ton annehmen. Obwohl der Architekt auf dem Aspekt der »italienischen Bergstadt« besteht, wirkt die Gebäudegruppe in der jetzigen Bauphase eher distanziert. Dieser Eindruck wird allerdings deutlich gemildert, wenn der Besucher die Esplanade vor dem Museum erreicht.

gante et éternelle, se dressant, sereine et idéale, sur la colline rocailleuse, sorte de structure aristotélicienne au milieu du paysage. Parfois, j'imagine que le paysage s'empare d'elle, parfois c'est elle qui se détache du paysage pour le dominer. Ils sont enlacés en un tendre dialogue, en une éternelle étreinte jusqu'à ne plus faire qu'un. Je reviens toujours aux architectes romains, à la villa d'Hadrien, à Caprarola, pour leur séquence d'espaces, leur lourde présence murale, leur sens de l'ordre et leur manière d'unir construction et paysage.»
Construit sur une colline imposante au-dessus de la San Diego Freeway, le Getty Center ressemble déjà à une forteresse ou à un monastère dominant Los Angeles, impression provenant en partie des murs de soutènement en travertin alvéolé. Cette pierre d'Italie qui introduit quelque chose de radicalement nouveau dans l'architecture de Richard Meier met en lumière le lien profond que celle-ci a toujours eu avec les monuments du passé. Diverses formes d'opposition venant du voisinage obligèrent l'architecte à abandonner pour cette fois les surfaces blanches. Même les panneaux en métal prennent ici une teinte beige clair. Malgré son insistance à présenter sa réalisation comme une «ville italienne sur la colline», celle-ci conserve son apparence distante qui s'atténue toutefois lorsqu'on arrive sur l'esplanade du musée.

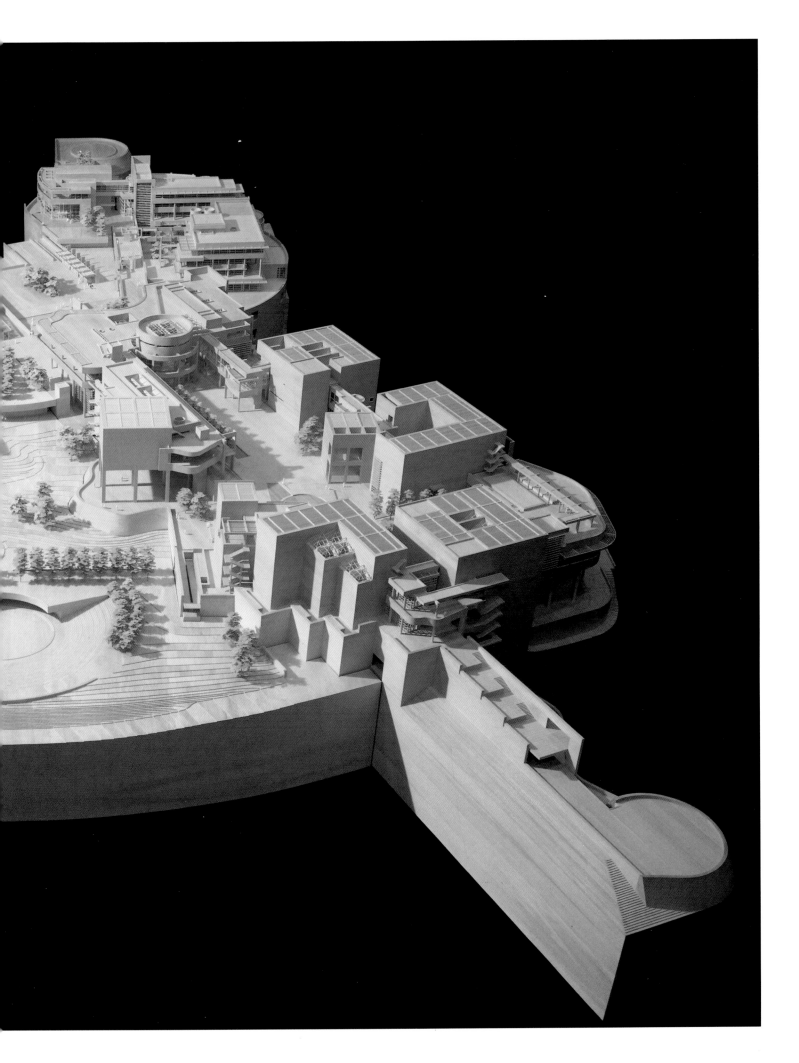

Chronological List of Buildings and Projects
Gebäude und Projekte in chronologischer Reihenfolge
Liste chronologique des projets et réalisations

1961–62
Lambert House
Fire Island, New York

1964
Monumental Fountain Competition, Benjamin Franklin Parkway, Philadelphia, Pennsylvania (with Frank Stella)

1965–67
Smith House
Darien, Connecticut

1963
Exhibition Design and Organization,"Recent American Synagoge Architecture",The Jewish Museum, New York, New York

1964–66
Renfield House
Chester, New Jersey (with Elaine Lustig Cohen)

1965
Rubin Loft Renovation
New York, New York

1963–65
Meier House
Essex Fells, New Jersey

1964–65
Studio and Apartment for Frank Stella
New York, New York

1966–67
Hoffman House
East Hampton, New York

1967–69
Saltzman House
East Hampton, New York

1969–71
House in Old Westbury
Old Westbury, New York

1971–73
Douglas House
Harbor Springs, Michigan

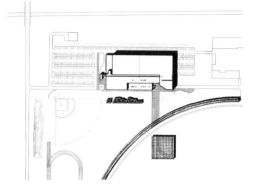

1968
Health and Physical Education Building, State
University College, Fredonia, New York

1969–72
Twin Parks Northeast Housing
Bronx, New York

1971
Olivetti Branch Office Prototype
Irvine, California; Kansas City, Missouri;
Minneapolis, Minnesota; Boston, Massachusetts;
Brooklyn, New York; Patterson, New Jersey

1969
Charles Evans Industrial Buildings
Fairfield, New Jersey and Piscataway, New Jersey

1970–77
Bronx Developmental Center
Bronx, New York

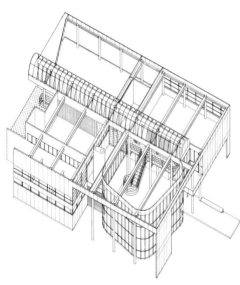

1971
Modification of the Olivetti Branch Office Prototype
Riverside, California; Albuquerque, New Mexico;
Tucson, Arizona; Fort Worth, Texas; Portland, Maine;
Memphis, Tennessee; Roanoke, Virginia

1969
House in Pound Ridge
Pound Ridge, New York

1971–76
Maidman House
Sands Point, New York

1971
Dormitory for the Olivetti Training Center
Tarrytown, New York

1974
Cornell University Undergraduate Housing
Ithaca, New York

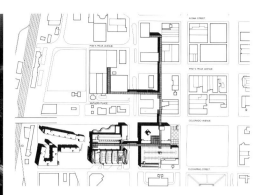

1976
Alamo Plaza
Colorado Springs, Colorado

1971
Olivetti Headquarters Building
Fairfax, Virginia

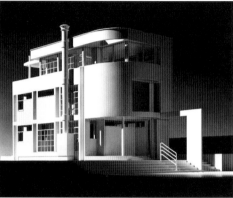

1976
Suburban Prototype House
Concord, Massachusetts

1972–74
Shamberg House
Mount Kisco, New York

1975–79
The Atheneum
New Harmony, Indiana

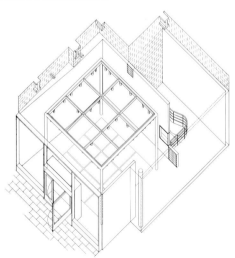

1976
Weber-Frankel Gallery
New York, New York

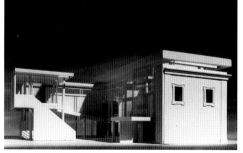

1973
Museum of Modern Art
Villa Strozzi, Florence, Italy

1975–78
Pottery Shed for the Robert Lee Blaffer Trust
New Harmony, Indiana

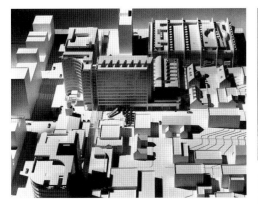

1977
Civic Center
Manchester, New Hampshire

1977–78
Palm Beach House
Palm Beach, Florida

1979–85
Museum for the Decorative Arts
Frankfurt/Main, Germany

1977
New York School Exhibition Structure
State Museum Albany Mall, New York

1978–82
Clifty-Creek Elementary School
Columbus, Indiana

1980
Condominiums
Beverly Hills, California

1977–78
Aye Simon Reading Room, Solomon R. Guggenheim
Museum, New York, New York

1978–81
The Hartford Seminary
Hartford, Connecticut

1979–83
Giovannitti House
Pittsburgh, Pennsylvania

1980–83
High Museum of Art
Atlanta, Georgia

1981
Renault Administrative Headquarters
Boulogne-Billancourt, France

1983–86
Westchester House
Westchester County, New York

1985–89
Grotta House
Harding Township, New Jersey

1982
Internationale Bauausstellung Housing
Berlin, Germany

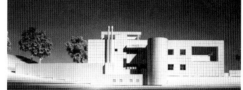

1983
Helmick House
Des Moines, Iowa

1984–89
Bridgeport Center
Bridgeport, Connecticut

1982–85
Des Moines Art Center Addition
Des Moines, Iowa

1983–
Designs for Swid Powell

1983–
Siemens Corporate Headquarters
Munich, Germany

1984–86
Ackerberg House
Malibu, California

1984–89
Siemens Office and Laboratory Complex
Munich, Germany

1985–97
The Getty Center
Los Angeles, California

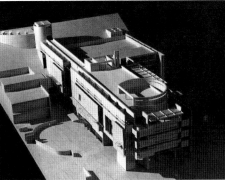

1987
The Eye Center Oregon Health Sciences University
Portland, Oregon

1987
Madison Square Garden Site Redevelopment
New York, New York

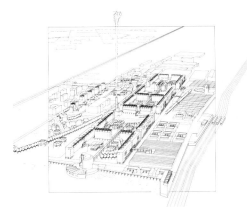

1986
Progetto Bicocca
Milan, Italy

1986–95
City Hall and Central Library
The Hague, The Netherlands

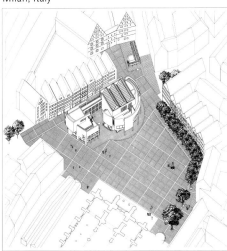

1986–93
Exhibition and Assembly Building
Ulm, Germany

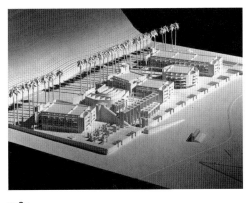

1987
Santa Monica Beach Hotel
Santa Monica, California

1987–92
Weishaupt Forum
Schwendi, Germany

1986
Rachofsky House I
Dallas, Texas

1987–92
Royal Dutch Paper Mills Headquarters
Hilversum, The Netherlands

1987–95
Museum of Contemporary Art
Barcelona, Spain

1988
Administrative and Maritime Center Master Plan
Antwerp, Belgium

1989
Office Building
Frankfurt/Main, Germany

1988
Cornell University Alumni and Admissions Center
Ithaca, New York

1988
Edinburgh Park Master Plan
Edinburgh, Scotland

1988–92
Canal+ Headquarters
Paris, France

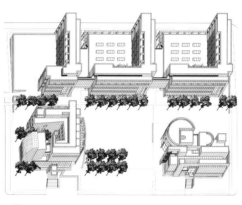

1989–93
Daimler-Benz Research Center
Ulm, Germany

1989
Museum of Ethnology
Frankfurt/Main, Germany

1988–94
Espace Pitot
Montpellier, France

1989
National Library of France
Paris, France

1989–93
Hypolux Bank Building
Luxembourg

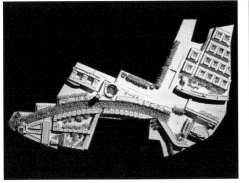

1990
Sextius Mirabeau Master Plan
Aix-en-Provence, France

1990—
Swiss Volksbank
Basel, Switzerland

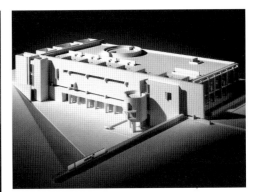

1991—95
Swissair North American Headquarters
Melville, New York

1990
Arp Museum
Rolandswerth, Germany

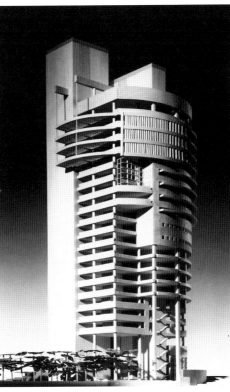

1990—
Grange Road Medical Center
Singapore

1992
Potsdamer Platz Master Plan
Berlin, Germany

1990—
Rachofsky House II
Dallas, Texas

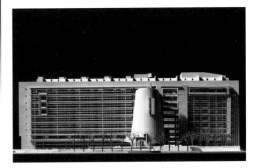

1993—
Federal Building and United States Courthouse
Islip, New York

Biography

1934 Born in Newark, New Jersey. The largest city in the state of New Jersey, Newark is located 10 kilometers from New York.

1952 Graduates from Columbia High School, which is located in Maplewood New Jersey, a quiet suburban community.

1957 Receives B. Arch. degree from Cornell University in Ithaca, New York. Meier has said that "Cornell was very free and open without any dominant influence... It was left up to the students and what they were interested in, to take advantage of a wide variety of opportunities for learning."

1959 Works for Davis, Brody & Wisniewski, New York.

1960 Works for Skidmore, Owings & Merrill, New York. SOM is known as one of the largest corporate architectural practices in the United States.

1961 Works in the office of Marcel Breuer, at the time when the Bauhaus master was undertaking the Whitney Museum project in New York. Of this period, which lasted until 1963, Meier has said, "Breuer was not influential although I worked for him for a while."

1965 One of Richard Meier's first completed projects was the house he built for his parents in Essex Fells, New Jersey. Completes Stella Studio and Apartment, New York. Meier's good friendship with the artist Frank Stella is one of the defining characteristics of his aesthetic approach.

1967 Completes the Smith House, Darien, Connecticut, which was to be a prototypical design for his later private

Richard Meier, 1977

residences. Approached via a bridge from the rear, closed side, and opening onto a generously glazed area overlooking Long Island Sound, the Smith House finds echoes throughout Meier's career.

1970 Undertakes the Bronx Developmental Center project, one of his first large, metal-panel buildings.

1973 Completes the Douglas House, Harbor Springs, Michigan. The gleaming white, ship-like presence of this house in its dramatic setting on a wooded hillside inspired numerous articles in the press and added to Meier's reputation.

1975 Visiting Professor of Architecture at Yale University, one of a large number of teaching assignments which he has accepted. Begins work on The Atheneum, New Harmony, Indiana.

1979 Begins work on the Museum for the Decorative Arts, on the banks of the Main in Frankfurt. This project represents a point of departure for Richard Meier because it was his first substantial European commission, and because he was confronted in a new way with the problem of the existing architectural con-

text, in the form of the 19th century Villa Metzler, integrated into the museum.

1980 Begins the High Museum of Art, Atlanta, Georgia, with its central atrium which is inspired by, and represents a critique of, Frank Lloyd Wright's Guggenheim.

1983 Competition entry for the Opéra Bastille, Paris. The anecdote has it that the jury for this anonymous competition thought they were choosing Richard Meier's project, but instead picked that of the relatively unknown Carlos Ott.

1984 Receives the Pritzker Prize, often described as the architectural equivalent of the Nobel. Begins work on the Ackerberg House, Malibu, California, and the Grotta House, Harding Township, New Jersey. Named officer of the French Ordre des Arts et des Lettres.

1985 Awarded the Getty Center project, a massive hilltop complex to be located above the San Diego Freeway in Los Angeles. This is certainly the largest commission given to a single architect for a cultural complex in the late twentieth century.

1986 Begins work on the Ulm Exhibition and Assembly Building and Hague City Hall and Central Library projects. Located very close to buildings by Rem Koolhaas, and Herman Hertzberger, the Hague City Hall is the centerpiece of the efforts of the municipality to renovate and animate the area around the Centraal Station. With the Getty Center progressing slowly, most of Richard Meier's work beginning at this point was in Europe. Relocates to larger offices at 475 Tenth Avenue in New York, partially as a result of his numerous European commissions.

1988 Recipient of the Royal Gold Medal, given by the Royal Institute of British Architects (RIBA). Begins the Museum of Contemporary Art, Barcelona, Spain, for completion in 1995.

1989 Undertakes Daimler-Benz Research Center, Ulm, Germany. Only three of the originally planned five or more buildings for this campus-like complex were to be built. Undertakes Museum of Ethnology, Frankfurt am Main, Germany for a site adjacent to the Museum for the Decorative Arts. Meier has described this project, subsequently delayed, as the design he regrets not building the most.

1992 Completes the Weishaupt Forum, Schwendi, Germany. Inspired by choice of Meier for the nearby Ulm Exhibition and Assembly Building, Max Weishaupt GmbH, a manufacturer of gas burners, asked the architect to build this nearly perfect gateway complex for their factory.

1993 Completion of the Ulm Exhibition and Assembly Building, and new design

Richard Meier, 1977

Hartford Seminary, Dedication June 7, 1981

for the Münsterplatz, reputed to be one of the most difficult sites in Germany. An outstanding example of the ways in which Richard Meier has succeeded in integrating his architecture into the delicate historic center of a European city.

1994 Begins design of new headquarters for Compaq Computers, Houston, Texas. This project may include Richard Meier's first relatively large tower. Completion of the Hague City Hall with the largest glassed atrium in Europe.

Biographie

Richard Meier in his New York office, 1986

1934 Geboren in Newark, New Jersey. Newark, die größte Stadt im Staat New Jersey, liegt 10 km von New York entfernt.

1952 Abschluß an der Columbia High School in Maplewood, New Jersey, einer ruhigen vorstädtischen Gemeinde.

1957 Architektendiplom an der Cornell University in Ithaca, New York. Meier sagt: »Cornell war sehr frei und offen, ohne irgendwelche dominierenden Einflüsse... Es stand den Studenten je nach ihren Interessen frei, eine große Vielfalt von Möglichkeiten für das Lernen zu nutzen.«

1959 Tätigkeit bei Davis, Brody & Wisniewski, New York.

1960 Tätigkeit bei Skidmore, Owings & Merrill, New York. SOM ist als eine der größten Architekturfirmen in den USA bekannt.

1961 Tätigkeit im Büro von Marcel Breuer, während der Bauhausmeister

am Projekt des Whitney Museum in New York arbeitete. Über diese Phase, die bis 1963 dauerte, sagt Meier: »Breuer hat keinen Einfluß auf mich ausgeübt, obwohl ich eine Zeitlang für ihn gearbeitet habe.«

1965 Eines von Meiers ersten realisierten Projekten ist das Haus, das er für seine Eltern in Essex Fells, New Jersey, baute. Fertigstellung von Stellas Studio und Appartement, New York. Meiers enge Freundschaft mit dem Künstler Frank Stella hat seine ästhetischen Vorstellungen stark beeinflußt.

1967 Fertigstellung des Hauses Smith, Darien, Connecticut, eines Prototyps seiner späteren Wohnbauten. Das Haus Smith ist über eine Brücke an der geschlossenen Rückseite zugänglich und öffnet sich auf einen großzügig verglasten Wohnbereich mit Ausblick auf den Long Island Sound. Elemente des Hauses Smith kehren in Meiers Schaffen immer wieder.

1970 Beginn des Projekts Bronx Developmental Center, eines seiner ersten großen, mit Metallplatten verkleideten Gebäude.

1973 Fertigstellung des Hauses Douglas, Harbor Springs, Michigan. Das strahlende, an ein weißes Schiff erinnernde Bild dieses Hauses in spektakulärer Lage auf einem bewaldeten Hügel führte zu einem starken Echo in der Presse und steigerte Meiers Ansehen.

1975 Gastprofessur für Architektur an der Yale University, einer von zahlreichen Lehraufträgen, die er übernahm. Beginn der Arbeit am Atheneum, New Harmony, Indiana.

1979 Beginn der Arbeit am Museum für Kunsthandwerk am Frankfurter Mainufer. Dieses Projekt stellte einen neuen Ausgangspunkt für Meier dar, weil es sein erster größerer Auftrag in Europa war, und weil er auf neue Weise mit dem Problem des vorhandenen architektonischen Umfeldes konfrontiert wurde – in Form der Villa Metzler aus dem 19. Jahrhundert, die in den Museumsbereich integriert wurde.

1980 Beginn der Arbeit am High Museum of Art, Atlanta, Georgia, mit seinem zentralen Atrium, das von Frank Lloyd Wrights Guggenheim Museum inspiriert ist und es zugleich kritisch interpretiert.

1983 Wettbewerbsbeitrag für die Opéra Bastille, Paris. Es heißt, daß die Jury für diesen Wettbewerb glaubte, sie hätte Richard Meiers Projekt gewählt. Tatsächlich jedoch entschied sie sich für den relativ unbekannten Carlos Ott.

1984 Erhält den Pritzker Prize, der häufig als Äquivalent des Nobelpreises

beschrieben wird. Beginn der Arbeit am Haus Ackerberg, Malibu, Calilfornia, und dem Haus Grotta, Harding Township, New Jersey. Wird zum Offizier des französischen »Ordre des Arts et des Lettres« ernannt.

1985 Auftrag für den Entwurf des Getty Center, eines umfangreichen Komplexes auf einem Berg über dem San Diego Freeway in Los Angeles. Dies ist sicherlich der größte Bauauftrag, den ein einzelner Architekt im späten 20. Jahrhundert für eine Kulturinstitution erhielt.

1986 Entwürfe für das Stadthaus Ulm und das Den Haager Rathaus mit Zentralbibliothek. Das Den Haager Rathaus liegt in der Nähe von Bauten Rem Koolhaas' und Herman Hertzbergers und bildet das Herzstück des städtischen Sanierungsplans für das Gebiet um die Centraal Station. Da das Getty-Projekt langsam voranging, verlagerte sich Richard Meiers Arbeit in dieser Zeit weitgehend auf Europa. Umzug in größere Büroräume an der Tenth Avenue 475 in New York, u. a. wegen der zahlreichen Aufträge in Europa.

1988 Erhalt der Royal Gold Medal des Royal Institute of British Architects (RIBA). Beginn der Arbeit am Museum für Zeitgenössische Kunst, Barcelona, das Anfang 1995 fertiggestellt werden soll.

1989 Arbeit am Daimler-Benz Forschungszentrum, Ulm. Nur drei der ursprünglich geplanten fünf oder mehr Bauten für diesen campusartigen Komplex wurden realisiert. Entwurf für das Museum für Völkerkunde, Frankfurt am Main, in der Nachbarschaft des Museums für Kunsthandwerk. Dieses Projekt, das später aufgegeben wurde,

bezeichnet Meier als das Gebäude, bei dem er am meisten bedauert, daß es nicht verwirklicht wurde.

1992 Fertigstellung des Weishaupt Forum, Schwendi. Durch Meiers Entwurf für das Stadthaus Ulm angeregt, beauftragt die Max Weishaupt GmbH, Hersteller von Gasbrennern, den Architekten mit dem Bau dieses Torkomplexes für die Fabrik.

1993 Fertigstellung des Ulmer Stadthauses und der Neugestaltung des Münsterplatzes, der architektronisch als einer der schwierigsten Orte in Deutschland gilt. Ein hervorragendes Beispiel für Meiers Fähigkeit, seine Architektur in das historische Zentrum einer europäischen Stadt zu integrieren.

1994 Entwurf der neuen Hauptverwaltung für Compaq Computers, Houston, Texas. Zu diesem Projekt wird wahrscheinlich Meiers erster, relativ hoher Turm gehören. Fertigstellung des Rathauses in Den Haag mit dem größten verglasten Atrium Europas.

Getty Center Design Unveiling, New York, 1991

Biographie

1934 Naissance de Richard Meier à Newark, New Jersey. Newark est la plus grande ville de l'Etat du New Jersey et se trouve à 10 km de New York.

1952 Diplôme de fin d'études de la Columbia High School (lycée) de Maplewood, tranquille commune suburbaine du New Jersey.

1957 Diplôme d'architecture à l'université de Cornell, Ithaca, New York. Pour Meier «Cornell était libéral et ouvert, sans influence dominante... Il ne tenait qu'aux étudiants de profiter de la grande variété des cours en fonction de ce qui les intéressait».

1959 Travaille chez Davis, Brody & Wisniewski, une agence d'architectes de New York.

1960 Entre chez Skidmore, Owings & Merrill, New York. Cette agence est l'une des plus grandes de ce type aux Etats-Unis.

1961 Travaille chez Marcel Breuer à l'époque où ce dernier réalisait son projet du Whitney Museum de New York. Meier juge ainsi cette période qui dura jusqu'en 1963: «Marcel Breuer n'eut guère d'influence sur moi bien que j'eusse travaillé pour lui quelque temps.»

1965 Un des premiers projets réalisés par Richard Meier est la maison de ses parents à Essex Fells, New Jersey. Réalise également le studio de Frank Stella à New York. L'amitié avec le peintre Stella joue un rôle déterminant dans son approche esthétique.

1967 Construit la maison Smith à Darien, Connecticut, qui deviendra une sorte de prototype de ses résidences privées futures. Accessible par un pont

Richard Meier, 1984

situé à l'arrière de la maison, fermée de ce côté et ouverte sur un espace presque entièrement vitré surplombant le Long Island Sound, la maison Smith servira de référence tout au long de la carrière de Meier.

1970 Entreprend la réalisation du Bronx Developmental Center, un de ses premiers grands édifices revêtus de panneaux en métal.

1973 Achève la maison Douglas à Harbor Springs, Michigan. Cette maison d'un blanc brillant aux allures de bateau, construite sur un site spectaculaire du lac Michigan, inspire de nombreux articles à la presse et accroît la réputation de Meier.

1975 Professeur associé d'architecture à l'université de Yale, un des nombreux postes d'enseignant qu'il a acceptés. Entreprend le projet de l'Atheneum, New Harmony, Indiana.

1979 Commence le projet du musée des Arts décoratifs de Francfort, au bord du Main. Projet important puisqu'il est sa première commande publique en Europe; de plus, il doit faire face pour la première fois à un contexte architectural difficile sous la forme de la villa Metzler datant du 19ème siècle et qu'il intègre au musée.

1980 Construction du High Museum of Art, Atlanta, Géorgie: l'atrium central est inspiré – et est en même temps la critique – du musée Guggenheim de Frank Lloyd Wright.

1983 Concours pour l'Opéra Bastille, Paris. Le jury de ce concours anonyme croit choisir le projet de Meier alors qu'il s'agit de la proposition d'un architecte bien moins connu, Carlos Ott.

1984 Lauréat du Prix Pritzker, considéré souvent comme l'équivalent du Prix Nobel en architecture. Projets de la maison Ackerberg à Malibu, Californie, et de la maison Grotta à Harding Township, New Jersey. Promu Officier de l'Ordre des Arts et des Lettres par le gouvernement français.

1985 Projet du Getty Center, un immense complexe situé sur une colline surplombant la San Diego Freeway «En quoi mes constructions sont américaines, même si elles sont réalisées en Europe? Elles ont quelque chose d'ouvert, de transparent, de clair qui est américain. Il y a aussi le rapport au site, le rapport entre la construction et la nature qui sont peut-être plus américains, mais à Los Angeles.» C'est certainement la plus grande commande de projet culturel attribuée à un seul architecte en cette fin de siècle.»

1986 Début des projets suivants: centre culturel et administratif d'Ulm, hôtel de ville et bibliothèque centrale de La Haye. Situé près des édifices construits par Rem Koolhaas et de Herman Hertzberger, l'hôtel de ville représente pour la municipalité la partie centrale de la rénovation et de la réanimation du quartier de la gare. Tandis que le Getty Center prend lentement forme, l'essentiel du travail de Meier s'effectue désormais en Europe. Transfère ses bureaux au 475 Tenth Avenue à New York pour traiter l'afflux des commandes en provenance d'Europe.

1988 Recoit la Médaille d'Or Royale du Royal Institute of British Architects RIBA; (Association des architectes britanniques). Début des travaux du musée d'Art contemporain de Barcelone, achèvement prévu pour 1995.

1989 Projet du centre de recherche Daimler-Benz, Ulm, Allemagne. Trois seulement des bâtiments de ce complexe genre campus sur les cinq ou plus prévus initialement verront le jour. Projet de musée ethnologique à Francfort, Allemagne, sur un site adjacent au musée des Art décoratifs. Meier décrit ce projet comme celui qu'il regrette le plus de n'avoir pu réaliser.

1992 Fin des travaux du Weishaupt Forum, Schwendi, près d'Ulm, Allemagne. Meier ayant été choisi comme architecte du centre administratif et culturel d'Ulm, l'entreprise Max Weishaupt GmbH, fabricant de brûleurs à gaz, demande à l'architecte de construire ce complexe quasi parfait qui sert d'accès à l'usine proprement dite.

1993 Achèvement du centre administratif et culturel d'Ulm et rénovation du Münsterplatz, réputé comme l'un des sites les plus délicats d'Allemagne. Exemple remarquable du savoir-faire de Meier, qui réussit à intégrer son architecture dans le centre historique complexe d'une ville européenne.

1994 Projet du nouveau siège de Compaq Computers, Houston, Texas, avec la tour la plus haute jamais réalisée par Meier.
Achèvement de l'hôtel de ville de La Haye doté du plus grand atrium vitré d'Europe.

Richard Meier in his New York office, 1993

Bibliography Bibliographie

Barthelmess, Stephan. *Richard Meier Collagen.* Includes: "The Collage in the Square: Art Parallel to Architecture" by Stephan Barthelmess. Germany: International Creative Management, March 1993.

Blaser, Werner. *Richard Meier: Building for Art.* Basel: Birkhäuser Verlag, 1990.

Blaser, Werner. *Weishaupt Forum/Richard Meier.* Includes Introduction by Richard Meier and Essay by Claudia Rudeck. Schwendi: Max Weishaupt GmbH, 1993.

Ciorra, Pippo, ed. *Richard Meier.* Includes "Richard Meier o la rappresentazione della modernità" by Livio Sacchi. Milan: Electa, 1993.

Costanzo, Michele et al. *Richard Meier/Frank Stella: Arte e Architettura.* Includes "Richard Meier and Frank Stella: a conversation about architecture and art". Milan: Electa, 1993.

Five Architects: *Eisenman/Graves/Gwathmey/Hejduk/Meier.* Introductions by Kenneth Frampton and Colin Rowe. New York: Wittenborn, 1972.

Galloway, David. *Der Dialog Als Programm Die Hypobank in Luxembourg.* Hypobank International S.A., 1993.

Gerace, Gloria, ed. *The Getty Center Design Process.* Introduction by Harold Williams, chapters by Bill Lacy, Stephen D. Rountree, Richard Meier. Los Angeles (CA): The J. Paul Getty Trust, 1991.

Izzo, Ferruccio and Alessandro Gubitosi. *Richard Meier Architetture/Projects 1986–1990.* Florence, Italy: Centro Di, 1991.

Pettena, Gianni, ed. *Richard Meier.* Venice: Marsilio, 1981.

Meier Richard. *On Architecture.* Text of Eliot Noyes Lecture. Cambridge (MA): Harvard University Graduate School of Design, 1982.

Meier, Richard. *Richard Meier, Architect: Buildings and Projects 1966–1976.* Introduction by Kenneth Frampton; Postscript by John Hejduk. New York: Oxford University Press, 1977.

Meier, Richard. *Richard Meier, Architect.* Introduction by Joseph Rykwert, Postscript by John Hejduk. New York: Rizzoli, 1984. Reprinted in Spanish. Barcelona, Spain: Editorial Gustavo Gili S.A., 1985.

Meier, Richard. *Richard Meier.* Includes the following: "Richard Meier and the City in Miniature" by Kenneth Frampton; "Richard Meier Interviews 1980–1988" by Charles Jencks; "RIBA Royal Gold Medal Address 1988" by Richard Meier. Great Britain: Academy Editions, 1990. German Edition. Stuttgart, Germany: Deutsche Verlags-Anstalt GmbH, 1990.

Meier, Richard. *Richard Meier Architect 2.* Includes the following: "Works in Transition" by Kenneth Frampton; "The Second Installment" by Joseph Rykwert; Postscript by Frank Stella. New York: Rizzoli, 1991.

Richard Meier: Stadthaus Ulm. Includes the following: "Richard Meier and the Urban Context" by David Galloway; "The Urbanization of Architecture" by Stephan Barthelmess. International Creative Management, 1993.

Richard Meier – The Getty Center. Includes the following: "A Citadel for Los Angeles and an Alhambra for the Arts" by Kurt Foster; "Richard Meier's Getty Center" by Henri Ciriani. *A+U*, November 1992 Special Issue.

Nesbitt, Lois E. *Richard Meier: Collages.* London: Academy Editions, 1990.

Nesbitt, Lois E. *Richard Meier Sculpture: 1992–1994.* New York: Rizzoli, 1994.

Vaudou, Valerie, ed. *Richard Meier.* Includes: "Avant-propos" by Richard Meier; "La Modernité comme seuil" by Hubert Damisch; "Radieuse modernité" by Henri Ciriani; "Sur Richard Meier" by Diane Lewis; "La capture du regard" by Jean Mas. Paris: Electa Moniteur, 1986. Reprinted in Italian. Milan: Electa, 1986.

Acknowledgements Danksagung Remerciements

The people listed here are among those who have worked in the office of Richard Meier & Partners and assisted on the buildings and projects in this book.

New York Office:

Kimberly Ackert
Stanley Allen
Jeff Barber
Roy Barris
Stuart Basseches
Margaret Bemiss
Thomas Bish
Peter Bochek
Patricia Bosch-Melendez
Ilana Brauner
Karin Bruckner
Andrew Buchsbaum
Peter Burns
Mary Buttrick
Ron Castellano
Pablo Castro-Estevez
Paul Cha
Christine Chang Hanway
Nancy Clark
Adam Cohen
Carlos Concepcion
Peter Coombe
Donald Cox
Charles Crowley
Jon Cooksey
Susan Davis-McCarter
Stephen Dayton
Allen Denenberg
David Diamond
Timothy Collins Douglas
Michael Duncan
John Eisler
Karin Elliot
Nikolaus Elz
Martin Falke
Peter Felix
Manfred Fischer
Renate Fischer
Patrick Flynn
Diederick Fokkema
Kenneth Frampton
Nina Freedman
Axel Gaede
Robert F. Gatje
Hans Goedeking
Kevin Gordon
Mark Goulthorpe
William Gravely
Lisa Green
W. Jeffrey Greene
Gerald Gurland
Kornel Gyamathy
Marc Hacker
Stephen Harris
Price Harrison

Brian Healy
Daniel Heuberger
Daniel Heyden
Katharine Huber
Raphael Justewicz
Gunter Kaesbach
Bernhard Karpf
Lucy Kelly
George Kewin
Jeffrey King
Grace Kobayashi
Christina Kohm
Robert Kravietz
Beat Küttel
Marianne Kwok
Ulrike Lauber
Robert Lewis
Hans Li
Eric Liebman
David Ling
John Locke
Renny Logan
Knut Luscher
Bernhard Lutz
Richard Manna
David Martin
Jonathan Marvel
Jean Mas
Mark Mascheroni
Siobahn McInerney
Petra Meerkamp
Brian Messana
Jean-Michel Meunier
Claude Meyers
Jun-ya Nakatsugawa
Marc Nelen
Alex Nussbaumer
Ana O'Brien
Alfonso Perez-Mendez
Matthew Petrie
Thomas Phifer
Katherine Platis
Vincent Polsinelli
Susan Price
Hans Put
John Quale
Jurgen Raab
Mihai L. Radu
Gilbert N. Rampy, Jr.
J. Gregory Reaves
John Reed
Rijk Rietveld
Peter Robson
Marc Rosenbaum
François Roux
Madeleine Sanchez

Arndt Sänger
Thomas Savory
James Sawyer
John Schneider
Rainer Scholl
Alan Schwabenland
Ralph Schwarz
Sandra Schwartz
Leonard Segel
Joseph Shields
Erin Shih
David Shilling
David Shultis
James Smith
Kimberly Smith
Gunther Standke
Ralph Stern
Daniel Stuver
Harley Swedler
William Talley
Steven Theodore
Stephen Tobler
Orestes Valella
David Walker
Wolfram Wöhr
Geoffrey Wooding
Evan Yassky
Dukho Yeon
Michael G. Yusem
François Zajdela
Birgit Zwankhuizen

Los Angeles Office:

Amy Alper
Robert Ashley
Greg Baker
John H. Baker
Donald E. Barker
Roger Barrett
John Bender
Peter Berman
Peter Blum
Manuel Bouza
Karen Bragg
Daniel Braun
Noel Carriere
Christopher Coe
Florencia Costa
James Crawford
Carlos Dell'Acqua
Victor Desantis
Joan Diengott
Maurice Edwards
Robert Edwards
Thomas Farrel
Nils C. Finne
Eric Fisher

Francis Freire
Tami Gan
Pavel Getov
Estabrook Glosser
Derek Gonzales
Paul Goodenough
Stefan Gould
Tom Graul
Michael Gruber
Jason Haim
Hiro Hemi
Bradley James Hill
Michael Hootman
Michael Hughes
Glen Irani
Richard Kent Irving
Bijoy Jain
Kam Kamran
Richard Kuhn
Robert Larson
Jean Lee
Wayne Martiny
James Matson
Hiroshi Matsubara
James Mawson
Stephen McCallion
Neil McLean
Marc McVay
Paul Mitchell
Milena Murdoch
John Murphey
Ronald Musser
Alexis Navarro
Kevin O'Brien
Olivia Ocampo
Jeri Oka
Carlo Paganuzzi
Michael Palladino
David Scott Parker
Martin Pease
John Petro
Ray Raya
Averill Schnider
Rivka Schoenfeld
Joanne Scott
Anne Seol
Timothy Shea
Lilia Skutnik
Jay Smith
Mark Sparrowhawk
Bruce Stewart
Richard Stoner
Krishna Suharnoko
Timothy Swischuk
Aram Tatikian
Phil Templeton

John Thomann
Russel N. Thomsen
Norma Title
George Todorovich
Jeffrey Turner
Stephen Vitalich
Thomas Vitous
Michael Volk
Phillip Warde
Bruce Weinstein
Malvin Whang
John Woell
Harry Wolf
Terrence Young
James Kinsun Yu
David Yuguchi

Photographic credits
Fotonachweis
Crédits photographiques